If you or someone you love has been ravaged by abuse, addiction, shame, crippling fear, or toxic secrets, Gina Cavallo's captivating and courageous account of her journey is the resource you need. This story of forgiveness, healing, and hope will bring restoration and encouragement to every reader.

CAROL KENT
Founder and Executive Director | Speak Up Ministries
Author | *When I Lay My Isaac Down*

Human trafficking is the scourge of our time. Through Gina Cavallo's powerful *A Survivor's Secrets*, you will be captivated by how Gina became a victim, got out of the system, and journeyed from trauma to freedom. I couldn't put it down!

RUTH GRAHAM
Author
Daughter of Billy Graham

Gina Cavallo is a rising leader on the issue of human trafficking. In *A Survivor's Secrets*, Gina opens her heart and delivers a powerful account of resiliency and determination. Her story will leave readers inspired and empowered to stand against human trafficking and support individuals who have survived it.

DR. DANIEL PAPA
President of the Board of Trustees | New Jersey Coalition Against
Human Trafficking

As you discover what Gina has overcome to find her identity—her worth, voice, purpose, and her empowerment—you will understand how she has come to be the agent of change she is today. *A Survivor's Secrets* will inspire anyone who has the courage to read it to see their own story through new eyes and do what's necessary to become who they were meant to be.

PHILLIP BRACCO, LMFT
Pastor of Care | Emergence Church, New Jers

T0036158

After hearing Ms. Gina Cavallo speak at an anti–human trafficking forum in my congressional district, I immediately invited her to provide her compelling testimony at the hearing I chaired on human trafficking in the US Congress. Gina is a courageous trafficking survivor and an expert who speaks with strength, experience, and authority about the human costs of this heinous crime. In *A Survivor's Secrets*, Gina offers hope to other victims as she draws on her faith and speaks of the healing that only God can provide. This book educates, motivates, and powerfully inspires. It's a must-read for anyone who wants to help trafficking victims hiding in plain sight.

CHRIS SMITH
US Congressman for New Jersey's 4th District

A Survivor's Secrets is a beacon of hope, reminding us that even in the face of unimaginable adversity, the human spirit can prevail.

ALFRED F. ABRAMSON
Retired Brigadier General | United States Army

Gina helps readers understand children who are misunderstood, abused, neglected, and disconnected. Shining a light on how secrets and lies groom children and make them vulnerable to the advances of predators, Gina gives caring adults a road map to recognize children like her.

PASTOR JO LEMBO
Director of Faith Initiatives | Shared Hope International

A Survivor's Secrets is a raw and beautiful book that brings the reader through the cobwebs of trauma, abuse, shame, and the imbalance of power that tried to tether Gina Cavallo to powerlessness and shame. You will be moved at how God's love triumphs over all the enemy's perversions.

TONYA TURNER
CEO & President | UNITAS

I lived most of my life within five minutes of where Gina grew up and lived and would have *never* imagined that what happened to her could happen in "my world." We can't be unaware of what goes on around us any longer! *A Survivor's Secrets* is a beautiful picture of how important it is to realize who we truly are. A must-read!

ROBERT F. DAVIS II
CEO | Christian Solidarity International & Odyssey Marketing and Advertising

In *A Survivor's Secrets*, Gina skillfully exposes the dark realities of human trafficking. She even found ways to sprinkle humor and show discretion when sharing the unimaginable truths of her lived experience. It's painful to see how "normal" childhood experiences can actually prime children for trafficking. The thought-provoking, raw details in this book will serve as a manual for parents and caregivers who are committed to doing everything in their power to effectively safeguard our children.

WINCEY TERRY-BRYANT
Singer, Songwriter, Playwright

A Survivor's Secrets has so much hope, truth, pain, life, and faith. Gina opens her heart and soul to the world by sharing her journey, and we all see that life is not solely about surviving our pain but choosing to thrive in spite of it—not only for ourselves but to benefit others who are still suffering.

TRICIA GRANT
Executive Director | Just Love Worldwide

A

SURVIVOR'S

SECRETS

Once Trafficked, Now Free from Feelings
of Worthlessness, Fear, and Shame

GINA CAVALLO

with Cindy Lambert

FOCUS
ON THE FAMILY.

A Focus on the Family resource
published by Tyndale House Publishers

30   29   28   27   26   25   24
7   6   5   4   3   2   1

To my Lord and Savior,
I know You don't call the qualified but qualify the called.
Thank You for breathing life into me and filling me with Your love,
grace, forgiveness, and purpose. Thank You for showing me who
I truly am in You, for taking my tragedies and turning them into
triumphs. I will forever honor You and give You all the glory.

CONTENTS

Part 1

PANDORA'S
BOX

2016

1

THE AWAKENING

I'D DRIVEN ONLY ABOUT A MILE OR TWO from the church when I realized my hands were trembling. I cranked up the heat, hoping the warmth would help calm me, even though I knew my shaking had nothing to do with the chilly evening air. I had to get a grip on my emotions. Panic. Grief. Horror. They had crashed through the wall that had held them back for so long. I shook my head to break free of them, but I could still feel them pulsing through my veins.

Had I known that attending my church's Redemption & Recovery group was going to rip open such old wounds, would I have started attending several weeks before? I had squirmed through the first few meetings, listening as others in the group shared their painful past experiences with trauma, alcohol, addiction, abuse, and the like. Yet in spite of my discomfort, I'd kept returning to the meetings, unable to resist the raw honesty of the people in my small group and the intensely personal way some of them were talking about Jesus. Maybe I felt a yearning to relate to Jesus the way they did. Or maybe it was a desire to connect with others on such a transparent level. Maybe the dark, hidden trauma of my past was aching to finally be exposed to the light. Or could it be that R&R might help free me from the pain of my past? Oh, how I longed for that freedom!

Well, whatever is drawing me back, I don't need it if it's going to make me feel like this. My heart was pounding so hard that I was finding it difficult to catch my breath. *I'm a mess!*

I'd come to Redemption & Recovery to serve coffee only as a way to support my son-in-law—the pastor—in the new ministry he'd launched at our church the fall of 2016. In fact, when he'd first mentioned the new program, he'd invited me to attend as a participant.

"Hey, Mom," he said, "why don't you join one of the women's recovery groups?"

I immediately got defensive. In fact, I felt irritated. I suspected he was trying to tell me that I needed to join because something was wrong with me. It seemed that people were always telling me what was wrong with me.

"No, thanks," I said, trying not to sound too insulted. "I don't need it." At the time I thought that R&R was only for people who struggled with alcohol and drugs—and those struggles were many years in my past.

"Well," he said, "I'm going to join one of the men's groups."

"Good for you. Maybe *you* need it." I regretted my sharp tongue the minute I heard my words. "But . . . maybe I could help by leading a group," I suggested, hoping to smooth any feathers I may have ruffled.

Wisely, he didn't press me for my qualifications or ridicule my offer. Instead, he enthusiastically filled me in on why he was launching the program.

"I believe this program is really going to change lives," he said. "We all have areas of our lives that God is calling us to grow in—areas where we can reflect Jesus and His power to save and heal and overcome. Areas like anger, resentment, codependency, loss, anxiety, grief, or addiction and substance abuse. R&R is for anyone seeking a safe place to remove masks and work through life's struggles in a deep way. This experience can really set people free."

Listening to his passion eased my defensiveness, and his mention of a safe place intrigued me.

"I could come and serve coffee," I offered, thinking perhaps he was politely ignoring my offer to lead a small group.

So that's how I started. But during the coffee breaks, several of the women were so welcoming that they soon coaxed me into joining their small group of about twelve. Being a people pleaser, I didn't want to seem unfriendly, so I reluctantly joined them. As I nervously sat in the circle, I was careful to maintain certain boundaries. It may have appeared to others that group conversation was easy for me, but the opposite was true. I often struggled trying to fit in with others. I always felt like I was on the outside looking in.

After attending R&R for about a month, I was listening to the women share their struggles one night when I began to sense that their stories were triggering some unwanted feelings in me. It was as if an invisible crowbar was prying the lid off a long-forgotten crate. My shoulders tensed and my stomach tightened. I tried to ignore the building anxiety by focusing intently on the woman who was talking at the moment. But then she started describing a traumatic experience. My breathing grew shallow. I realized that I'd clenched my teeth. Then a very old memory came to mind.

Something I hadn't thought about in decades. The memory made me flinch.

No! I'm not going there. Nothing good will come of it.

I wanted to leave right then, but I didn't want to seem rude or hurt the feelings of the woman speaking. So I did everything I could to distract myself. I scanned the room and counted heads. I counted ceiling tiles. I tried to go numb. But the crowbar was still working on that box, the emotional pressure inside me threatening to escape. Long-forgotten memories were now springing to mind, and with them came feelings of panic. When the session was over, I bolted from my chair and tore out of the building to my car.

But the onslaught of old memories wouldn't stop. On the way home, I was trembling as I tried to focus my full attention on driving. I checked my speed. Took note of the distance between my car and the car in front of me. Eyed the rearview and side mirrors. Turned on my favorite music. Anything to distract myself from the images swirling in my mind.

I'll be home in a few minutes, I assured myself, in spite of the typical New Jersey traffic. *This will pass.*

Suddenly a face I hadn't seen in forty years flashed through my mind. The angry face of a man only inches from my own and wearing a look of disgust. I saw him pushing me backward and slapping me across the face so hard that I fell to the floor.

Oh, dear God, don't let me go there.

But it was too late. The past was screaming its way into the present, and I was coming undone.

•　•　•

I pulled into the driveway, turned off the ignition, and fought to take a few deep breaths. I knew my husband, Peter, would be occupied watching television in the living room. I could easily avoid getting involved in a conversation.

"How were things at the church?" Peter called to me as I hung up my jacket.

"Fine," I called back as I moved toward the bedroom to change. "It was a good night." Confidentiality was a priority at R&R, so Peter knew not to expect me to say more.

It was comforting to be home, to hear Peter's voice, to be reminded that I had a good and happy life now. But it didn't feel good to keep a secret from Peter about my experience that night. My silence felt like a lie. But what choice did I have? Peter knew nothing of my old life. We'd been married for four years, and these memories had remained buried where they belonged. It was as if they were secrets I'd been keeping even from myself. No reason to dig them up, right?

But somehow I knew it wasn't right at all. And I wasn't *trying* to dig them up. These forgotten memories were escaping all on their own, and they truly frightened me.

Just then an image of myself cowering from an oncoming punch flashed before me. *Where is all this coming from?* I wondered. I was terrified. *What is wrong with me?* I wanted to believe this was just a bad dream that would go away. But I knew in my gut that these memories were real. Actual events from the past were haunting me, and I couldn't control or stop them. Attending Redemption & Recovery had triggered them. How was it possible I had suffered something so inhumane and then buried it so deeply?

I'll just not go back to R&R, I thought. *The memories will fade again.*

I wanted to run into the living room and tell Peter what was happening. After all, isn't that what you're supposed to do in a marriage—be honest and transparent and feel completely safe, especially with your best friend?

Wrong! cried a voice from deep inside. *The last time I told a husband of mine the truth about my past, the cost was too high.* And with that thought came a flashback of my first marriage, which had been to a man named Ray. With him I'd learned the hard way what happens when you reveal an ugly past to a husband. But that's a story for later.

• • •

I pulled myself away from the memory of Ray and climbed into bed, even though it was earlier than my normal bedtime. Later, when Peter came to bed and snuggled up next to me, I pretended to be asleep. But I was far from it. The old memories still haunted me. My pillow was damp with tears, my palms sweaty, my teeth clenched, and my stomach in knots.

Since leaving the church that evening, I'd been accosted by faces, names, scenes, sounds, smells, and images all locked away in my soul long ago. I'd thought those memories were dead, but now I knew they'd just been lying in wait. The memories poured from Pandora's box, and there would be no gathering them up and burying them again.

Something about the Redemption & Recovery group had pierced me. Shame had scorched me. Truth had nauseated me. Panic had overwhelmed me. Fear had moved into my heart and taken over.

What would Peter think if he knew about my past? How could he ever understand? I could barely wrap my head around that three-year nightmare, something so foul that it had robbed me of all my dignity, so inhumane that it had left me deeply shamed and traumatized. No wonder I'd blocked it out of my memory.

Now that the memories had resurfaced, I wanted to find the cleansing and peace that the leaders of R&R had been speaking of. But how could I? Dare I even utter my experiences to them? How would they react? Would they tell others? What would my daughter say? My son-in-law? I'd lose everything. I'd lose them and my church and Peter—the dearest gifts in my life. I could even lose myself. What if I began drinking again? What if I sank back into the darkness of depression, the suicidal state that had once nearly claimed my life?

Dear God, I'm so afraid. I can't go back there.

But I was already on the threshold, and stepping forward seemed inevitable.

Finally I drifted into a fitful sleep.

I spent the next day pretending nothing had happened. And the following days as well. I skipped out on R&R for several weeks, calling the leader and saying that my schedule had too many conflicts and I couldn't help with coffee anymore or return to the small group.

I expected to feel relief. With no R&R sessions, surely the memories would die down. But far from it. They continued to haunt me. Horrendous scenes kept popping into my mind. Faces. Threats. Beatings. The feel of a knife being held to my back. Knowing my abuser slept with a gun under his pillow. And the burning shame at the unspeakable things I had been forced to do. It seemed like the more I tried to stuff the memories back into the past, the more they multiplied. It was terrifying to realize I had no control over the flashbacks.

Then one afternoon my phone rang. It was Marianne, my R&R small-group leader. She'd been trying to reach me for weeks, but I'd ignored her calls until now. I'm not sure what prompted me to answer this time, but I did. After some polite small talk, she got to the point.

"Look, Gina, I don't know what you're going through, and that's okay. I don't need to know. But we miss you and want you back in our group. And whatever you're going through, I want you to know that you are safe with us. You are safe here. Please don't be afraid. Please come back."

Safe? I'm safe? And they miss me?

Her words were like cool, fresh water pouring into my thirsty soul. I drank them in and wanted more. My past, my memories, my shameful secrets—they all felt so dangerous and threatening to everything I held dear. *Safety* was precisely what I longed for. It was what I needed. I thanked Marianne for calling and told her I'd consider returning.

But I knew that if I was going to do this—if I was going to participate in this recovery program and revisit my dark past—I'd need more than just this small group. I'd likely need a professional counselor as well, someone who could help me work through the trauma. This was too dark and deep to face without a counselor's guidance. I also understood that I'd have to tell Peter everything about my past. If I was going to tell my small group and my counselor, then my husband needed to know as well.

So I made my decision. My shame had had the upper hand for too long. I wouldn't let it control me any longer. I believed that God wanted to free me from this dark fear. He'd brought me to Redemption & Recovery for a purpose, and it was finally time to face my fears, expose my brokenness, and find healing.

God, help me, I prayed as I parked my car and walked into the church.

2

A SAFE PLACE

MARIANNE SAW ME AS I ENTERED the church lobby. She walked over and gave me a warm hug. Other group members also made their way to me, welcoming me back with genuine smiles and kind words. No one asked why I'd missed the recent sessions. They simply let me know they were glad to see me. The kind welcome calmed my nerves.

At my church, Redemption & Recovery meets for about two hours each week. (This program and its materials are known in many other churches by the published name *Celebrate Recovery*.) For the first hour, everyone meets together in a large group for worship and then either a lesson or a testimony. For the second hour, we split into separate rooms, where we gather in small groups called "open share groups." Men and women each have their own groups, and in these more intimate circles, we discuss that evening's lesson or testimony or anything we may want to share about how we're doing. Then on another night of the week, we have what are called "step studies," where we discuss the homework we've done in our workbooks.

Given how panicked I'd been when I'd left small group several weeks before, I expected to be extremely anxious that evening. To my surprise, I wasn't. I sensed a real peace at being back and an anticipation of what God might have in store. I also took comfort in recalling Marianne's words that I'd be safe and wouldn't have to speak if I didn't want to. I could just . . . listen.

Safe was an alluring word for me. For as long as I could remember, I'd always wanted to feel truly safe. One of the reasons I'd fallen in love with Peter in my late fifties was that he was the safest man I'd ever known. I knew he would never hurt me or try to control or fix me. But I also knew that in my fifty-some years I'd grown so accustomed to keeping dark secrets that I just kept on keeping them, even from this man I trusted.

Frank Warren, author of the bestselling PostSecret series of books, once said, "There are two kinds of secrets. The ones we keep from others and the ones we keep from ourselves."[1] I kept both kinds. A nearly three-year ordeal in my early twenties had traumatized me so deeply that I'd buried the memories, keeping them secret even from myself.

Peter and I married in 2012, four years before my "awakening" at Redemption & Recovery. Those four years had been the safest years of my life.

I never felt safe as a child—not in my home, at school, or in the nice suburban neighborhood I lived in. During my teen and young-adult years, my desire to escape those environments drove me into the most unsafe relationships imaginable. As I emerged from those years, I was so unstable and self-destructive that I wasn't even safe from myself. In subsequent years, I began to believe that real safety was impossible to find. I couldn't find it in the Catholic church of my childhood, in my two failed marriages, in any of several employment opportunities, or even—sometimes—with the police.

Marianne had unknowingly tapped into one of the greatest longings of my life when she'd said that R&R would be a safe place for me. This promise of safety—an elusive, dreamlike ideal—was a large part of what had motivated me to take the risk and return to the group. That and the fact that my old memories were now traumatizing me.

One principle they teach at R&R is to avoid comparing stories. Early on I found that to be a challenge. As some women shared their trauma and heartbreak over abuse they'd suffered, I couldn't help but wonder what the effect would be of describing my own experiences, some of which seemed far more horrific. *Are my secrets too ugly for these women?* I wondered.

I wasn't sure. But as I witnessed the empathy and caring between the women, I gradually understood the real comfort and safety the group offered. While I wasn't yet ready to share my own story, I felt hopeful that I might one day be on the receiving end of that kind of security. Empathy had never been a part of my childhood or my young adulthood, and because of the shame I carried with me from those years, I'd never risked sharing my pain with others. What would it be like if I truly believed that sharing could be safe?

As I silently observed the women in my small group, I found myself looking forward to meeting in a few days with a counselor I had found who might help me walk through the process of recovery. *Will I find comfort and safety there?*

Over the next several weeks, with my counselor and in my R&R group, I began testing the waters. Without explaining the big picture of my past, I shared some incidents that had involved violence and abuse. Ever so slowly, week after week, I opened up a little more. There was no judgment. I *was* safe with these people. I was cared for and affirmed. My courage grew.

My counselor was the first to hear the breadth of my story and the depth of my darkest secrets. His responses were exactly what I needed. Encouraged and emboldened, I disclosed a bit more to my small group. My fear was slowly melting away, yet at the same time, I felt a growing discomfort knowing that I'd told near strangers a few of my painful experiences but had not yet told my husband.

"I've decided I'm ready to tell Peter," I said to my counselor a few weeks after I began opening up to the group. "I've already shared parts of my story with the women in my small group. I'm going to go through with this program. I'm determined to finish it. But since I've told them, I just have to tell my husband. And I want to tell him sooner rather than later."

His hand popped up like a stop sign. "Well, hold on for a minute, Gina," he said. "Let's prepare you for those conversations. Let's work through this over a few more sessions."

So I reluctantly agreed to hold off. That was on a Thursday. But on Saturday morning, I awoke feeling strongly that I was ready. I didn't want to keep things from Peter for even one more day. It was time to make the leap.

As we often did on Saturday mornings, Peter and I each grabbed a coffee and headed into the living room to chat about our weekend. I sat on the couch just a few feet from Peter's chair. The sun was streaming in the window behind me, warming my back. The warmth was comforting. To my surprise, a sense of peace descended on me. No, it didn't take away my fear. I was still aware that it was possible I was about to lose everything. Several weeks had passed since I'd joined the R&R group, and four decades since

I'd uttered a word to anyone else about the events that had so traumatized me. But at this point peace overshadowed my fear, and I knew that I was ready to move forward no matter the cost.

Somehow I sensed that God was with me, and it was time to step out and trust Him in a way I'd never trusted Him before. I sensed Him telling me, *I've got you, Gina. Don't be afraid.* I felt an overwhelming peace that, regardless of the outcome, God held me safely in His grip. I'd lived in fear my whole life, so when I sensed God telling me not to be afraid, I nearly jumped at the opportunity.

"I want to talk to you about something," I said in a voice so calm, so relaxed, that I marveled at the sound of it.

Peter simply took a sip of his coffee and sat back, clearly ready to listen, no concerns written on his face. For a moment, I wasn't sure where to begin. I hadn't rehearsed this in my mind. I didn't have any points planned out in advance. I had no idea how to even tell my story. It seemed too big. Too sprawling. Too complex.

"I will totally understand if you can't deal with this," I heard myself say. "If you can't, and you ask me to go, I will go. I won't fight for anything."

Poor Peter. His face went from relaxed and mellow to fear stricken. His eyes grew large, and his brow furrowed as he sat there with his legs crossed and his arms folded. I realized I needed to spill this out fast—at least some part of it. I could go back and fill in the details later, but I had to get right to the point.

"It's about my past. Way before you."

Peter's face relaxed just a bit. His look of fear melted into one of concern—and tenderness.

"After high school," I started, and then I paused. How could I possibly fit my entire nightmare into a few words?

But then the words came gushing out so fast that I could barely take a breath.

As I spoke, I watched Peter's face fall. Tears filled his eyes and spilled down his cheeks, but he didn't move or make a sound. I braced myself for the worst—that Peter was already planning to leave me—but there was no stopping me now. I somehow found myself putting words to the nightmare that had held me prisoner for so long.

The floodgates had opened, and my story was tumbling out in a powerful, overwhelming rush. I spoke things I'd never spoken—not ever, not to anyone—and as I did, my imprisoned heart, long bound in fear, pain, and worthlessness, spewed out ugly secrets it had been holding for so terribly long.

Part 2

EASY PREY

1972–1973

3

BETRAYAL

I SAT ON THE SAGGING MOTEL MATTRESS and stared at the phone on the nightstand wondering when I'd finally get an answer from Charlie. This was day four. How much longer would I be alone in Miami waiting for him to arrive? The excitement I'd felt when I arrived in town was giving way to anxious loneliness. I needed to hear his reassuring voice. I needed to know when he'd be arriving from New Jersey to join me, as he'd promised.

It hadn't been long since I'd graduated from high school, and I was eager to get started on our life together in Florida—to find an apartment and go job hunting and get settled in. I'd chosen this little motel because it fit my meager budget and was close to the airport where I'd landed. But it was looking shabbier by the day, and I was growing impatient with nothing to do but watch television and wait for the phone to ring. Without a car or much money, I could think of nothing else to do.

I pulled the phone onto the bed next to me, took a deep breath, and dialed Charlie's number, hoping I was about to hear his voice. My heart leaped when, on the third ring, he answered.

"Charlie! I'm so glad I caught you. When are you coming?"

There was a momentary pause, and then I heard a sound I least expected. *Laughter.* Not warm laughter, either. It was *cutting.*

"Coming?" Charlie said with a snicker. "Don't tell me you're really in Florida waiting for me!" He paused for a moment as if waiting for me to answer. Then with derision dripping from his voice, he said, "You actually believed me? Are you really that stupid?"

An icy chill swept over me. I couldn't breathe. I wanted to believe he was teasing me, that any moment he'd change his tone and reassure me that he couldn't wait to see me. But my hope died when I heard that word: *stupid.*

It was a word that had been thrown at me my entire life.

From my earliest years, I'd heard it from my older siblings. "Hey, Mom, did you hear what Gina said?" Or "You are so stupid and retarded," they'd say, laughing in my face when they saw the Fs on my report cards.

I'd hear it from classmates talking to one another when I was held back in school because I couldn't keep up. "Don't hang with Gina. She's stupid."

I'd hear it from my mother whenever we were having company. "Don't talk in front of our guests, Gina. You sound stupid when you talk. It's embarrassing."

And my father implied it when we visited the expensive private school one of my sisters attended and I said, "I can't wait until I'm old enough to come here."

"Only smart students with good grades get to come to this school," Dad had said.

Until this moment, Charlie had never called me stupid. Now he had. And I knew he meant it. I was cut to the core, and nausea crept up on me.

"But you said you wanted to move to Florida with me. You said to go ahead, and you'd follow in a few days. I spent almost all my money getting here. And I've been here waiting for you."

I was embarrassed hearing my own words. I sounded pathetic and I knew it. I'd been tricked. Charlie had just wanted to get rid of me, and I'd fallen for his plan.

I *was* stupid.

I couldn't go back to New Jersey. For one thing, I'd lied to my parents about my reason for moving to Florida. I told them I was going to nursing school and never mentioned my plans with Charlie. My Italian Catholic parents were very protective, and I'd never been allowed to make decisions or choices about my own life. I longed to be independent, to be my own boss. So I wasn't about to return home to look like a foolish failure.

Home had never been a happy place for me.

* * *

Since graduating from high school the year before, I had been at odds with my father about my career choices. My heart's desire had been to become an airline stewardess (as they were called in the seventies). I enjoyed people, wanted to travel, and saw it as a glamorous career, but my father saw it as a position where men would take advantage of me and where I would gain a tarnished reputation. So he had forbidden me from pursuing that dream.

Ironically, he approved of my second choice: modeling. John

Robert Powers School of Modeling was near our home, and one of the members of our church was an instructor there. This evidently influenced my father's positive opinion of the place. All went well until it was time to develop a portfolio. The school provided referrals to outside agents and photographers. It wasn't long before I discovered that my agent, a guy about twice my age, expected me to tolerate creepy sexual innuendo and inappropriate touching as he "brushed" past me.

Appalled and totally unequipped to respond, I tried to ignore his advances by moving out of touching range and pretending that I hadn't noticed. He'd act as if nothing had happened and would just go about business as usual. He was always so in charge, larger than life and in complete control of the room. I felt outpowered and awkward, like a child in a man's world. His behavior seemed like an unspoken, unacknowledged game, and I loathed being alone in a room with him. But I said nothing—to him or to anyone else. I had a long history of keeping secrets, so I just tried to manage the situation as best as I could, always squirming to keep an arm's distance between us. He repulsed me, but I tried to act professional, as if everything were normal.

My agent was enough to deal with; then one day my photographer made extremely inappropriate sexual advances while I was alone with him doing a photo shoot for my portfolio. When I rebuffed him, he angrily informed me that if I complained, he'd see to it that I'd never get any work in the profession again. I believed him. The experience deeply rattled me, but again I said nothing to anyone.

When my portfolio was completed, my agent helped me land some modeling work on a few runway jobs and magazine shoots. On the one hand, I was thrilled. I soon learned, however, that my weight would be constantly criticized. I was pressured to lose pounds quickly by not eating. But it was never enough. Desperately wanting to please and excel, I slipped into anorexia until I found myself ill and hospitalized. There, away from the daily sexual pressure and disapproval over my weight, I more clearly recognized the stress I'd been under. I decided the modeling life wasn't for me. Once discharged from the hospital, I never considered modeling work again.

• • •

After modeling, I set my sights on a career in health care. One day I had an interview at a large facility that housed a veteran's home and a psychiatric facility. I arrived and parked but was uncertain which entrance to use. A man parked nearby noticed me and said, "You seem lost." He was tall and well dressed, and he seemed kind.

"Yes, I'm not sure which entrance to use. I'm trying to find the personnel department."

"Oh, I'll show you," he said.

Some part of me knew better than to trust a total stranger sitting in a parked car, but I followed him inside. He led me to a closed, unmarked door and held it open for me. I stepped into the room, and he followed close behind me, shutting and locking the door. This clearly wasn't the personnel office. I saw a chair and a bed. It looked like the sleeping quarters for an intern or something. Immediately an alarm went off inside me. But before I could process what was happening, he overpowered me and pushed me onto the bed, slapping his large hand over my nose and mouth so I could barely breath—and certainly not scream. Then he raped me.

Afterward he fled the room.

The entire incident happened in mere minutes. Deeply shaken and dazed, I just wanted to escape the room. The attack triggered a similar memory from my childhood. With all these horrific images flashing through my mind, I hid my torn panties in my pocketbook, smoothed my skirt, and ran from the building to my car.

Overwhelmed with feelings of deep shame, I told no one of the incident. I never returned to the facility, and I would never learn whether the man was a doctor, an employee, or an outpatient. As was my habit with similar traumas during my childhood, I stuffed the hideous ordeal deep down inside—where I would keep all my other dirty secrets.

●   ●   ●

I met Charlie in a bar where he was the bartender. Our relationship soon became sexual. I'd been itching for independence, and Charlie made me feel loved, wanted, and special—something I'd never felt at home. A few months after meeting Charlie, I left home against my parents' wishes and moved in with him.

Several months later, Charlie surprised me with the idea of taking off for Florida together. I found the idea adventurous and romantic. It also suited my desire to break away from my family. So, with no planning whatsoever, I leaped at the opportunity. I ached to show everybody that I wasn't the stupid failure they painted me to be. A daring and independent new start in Florida would show them all! So I told my parents the lie about pursuing a nursing career, bought my ticket, and boarded the plane headed for my new life, totally clueless as to what I was getting into.

Now, duped and alone in a shabby motel, I berated myself for being just as stupid as everyone had always told me I was. *One failure after another.* Though heartbroken over Charlie's betrayal and deeply shamed at being fooled, I was not going to crawl home to my family. That's what they'd be expecting. I was determined to prove that I could succeed independently. I even told myself that this experience would make me stronger.

Still, there was reality to deal with. I was about out of money and needed a place to live and then a job. I had a godmother in nearby Pembroke Pines. Though she was only about eight years older than me, my parents had chosen her for the role at my confirmation in the Catholic Church. When I was a child, she lived close by and would always spend time with me, taking me shopping or to special events. I saw her as an ideal older sister, role model, and best friend. I was still a child when she moved to Florida, but we stayed close in spite of the miles. Now I called her, and she warmly invited me to stay with her until I got my feet under me.

I quickly landed two part-time jobs—one at an Avis, the car rental company, and one as a waitress in a nearby Italian restaurant called Doria's. I was proud of myself. *I can do this.*

Determined to manage the hurt and anger I felt toward my family, I avoided phone contact with my parents. A few months later I discovered that my godmother had been updating her mother about my activities, and her mother (a very close friend of my mom's) was passing along the information to my parents. Not wanting my family to continually monitor me, I moved into an apartment with a new roommate. I was making ends meet and ever so slowly saving a meager amount of money.

I hadn't yet developed a long-term plan, and as much as I told myself I wanted to be free of my family, the truth was that my goals revolved around them. I desperately wanted to make myself successful so I could eventually go home and show my family that I wasn't the stupid failure of a daughter or sister they believed I was. I yearned to be acknowledged, to be respected, to belong, to be loved. Gaining my financial independence was a huge part of the image I hoped to project.

Waitressing suited me, and chatting with regular customers was, as far as I was concerned, a perk of the job. One regular lunch customer, Hank, was especially warm and friendly. He was about my dad's age—in his fifties—and told me more than once that I reminded him of his daughter. Over time I thought of him as sort of a father figure, though with a far gentler spirit than my own dad. Whenever he entered Doria's, which was quite often, I always brightened and made sure I was the one who served him. He was kind and showed what seemed like a fatherly interest in me. I enjoyed our small talk as I served him lunch and refilled his coffee cup. Being around Hank always made me feel safe.

December came, and one day as I poured his coffee, he asked, "So, what are you doing for the holidays? Going home?"

"Oh no. I'm not planning on going home," I said.

"Well, don't you think your parents will miss you?" Hank clearly didn't know about my painful background.

"Well, I don't want to go home until I'm ready."

Then he asked a question that really made me pause. "What do you have to be ready for?"

"Oh, I want to go home when I can show them I'm successful. I want to show them I'm doing great."

"Well, what does that look like?" Hank asked.

"When I go home for Christmas, I want to bring them nice gifts." In my mind, gift giving would show my love and win their acceptance. "Right now, I can afford to either get them all gifts or buy a plane ticket. But I can't afford both. But in time, that's what I'm gonna do."

Hank took a swallow of coffee and paused as if in thought. "I'll tell you what," he finally said. "What if I give you the money for the plane ticket, and you use your own money to buy them gifts?"

I couldn't believe he'd say such a thing. "What? Why would you do that for me?"

"I'm doing it for you because I have a daughter," he said. "I would want to see my daughter, so I'm sure your family wants to see you. If you can pay me back someday, fine. If not, no worries."

I was so moved that I didn't think twice. I said okay.

"I've got to run now, but I'll be back with the money," he said.

I floated through the rest of the day, imagining the gifts I'd buy and the looks of shock on my four siblings' faces. Would Dad beam with pride? Would Mom be proud of me? As the afternoon faded, I kept my eye on the door, hoping Hank would come soon. Finally my shift ended in the late afternoon. *Maybe he'll come tomorrow,* I thought. I grabbed my pocketbook and stepped outside.

I heard a horn blow and looked across the street. There, in the small lot, I saw Hank sitting in his car. He waved me over. Excited he'd really come back, I crossed the street and stepped up to his window.

"Come around and get in," he said.

I did as I was told and slid into the front passenger seat. I was really touched that he'd be so generous. No one had ever done anything like that for me before.

"Here you go," Hank said, holding out the money. I took it.

Suddenly two police cars pulled up close on either side of us. Uniformed officers were jumping out of the cars and yelling, "Police! Step out of the car!" They scared me to death. It took me a moment to realize that they were yelling at me.

"What's going on?" I was saying when one officer yanked open my door and grabbed my arm. Before I knew what was happening, I was spun around facing the car, and handcuffs were roughly slapped onto my wrists. Now I was crying and trembling and choking out the words "What's happening?"

"You're under arrest for prostitution," one officer said. I could see that Hank, too, was out of the car on the other side, surrounded by officers, but I couldn't hear what was going on over there. I did hear one of the officers shout another word: *solicitation.* But I didn't know what that meant either.

"What?" I cried out. "What's that?" *Prostitution. Solicitation.* At the time, I literally didn't know the meanings of these words.

"Why is this happening?" I asked, sobbing. "What did I do?" But no one answered me.

An officer took my arm, pulled me over to a police car, opened the back door, and ordered, "Get in."

Terror tore through me, but I shut up and did as I was told. My head was spinning, everything was moving so fast. I couldn't catch my breath and felt faint. I couldn't see Hank. All I saw were uniforms around the police car. Then two officers climbed into the front seat, and the car started moving forward. Totally overwhelmed, confused, and terrified, I sat completely still, quietly weeping.

4

THE BAILOUT

AS I RODE IN THE BACK SEAT of the police car, the only sounds I heard were the police radio and my own quiet weeping. We didn't drive far before coming to a stop, and I found myself being led, handcuffed, into the Hollywood, Florida, police station. What came next was a blur. Some officer offered to let me make a phone call, but I was in such a state of shock and panic that I could think of no one to call, so I declined.

After my fingerprints and photograph were taken, I was led to a large cell that held a small number of women, some sitting on cots, some leaning against the walls, a few pacing around. The smell of sweat and body odor and old cigarette smoke and alcohol hung in the air. I found a place along a cinder block wall, leaned against it, and withdrew into myself, doing my best to disappear.

The door clanked shut, sending a shudder through me. By this point I felt nothing but numbness. I spoke to no one, and no one spoke to me.

I don't know how much time passed. It felt like many hours. Eventually my legs grew weary, and I just let myself slide down the wall until I sat on the cement floor. My mind cleared a little, and I started trying to make sense of what had happened. What about Hank? Had he been arrested too? Why did so many police show up? And what did *solicitation* and *prostitution* mean? I felt like I had back in school—stupid—for not knowing a word.

I'm not the brightest crayon in the box, I reprimanded myself, rehearsing in my mind what I'd heard said about me more than once. *I must be everything they said I was—stupid and retarded.*

Finally, after what must have been hours, an officer appeared and called my name. I stood, and he motioned for me to come to the cell door as he unlocked it.

"Your friend is here to get you out," he said.

Friend? What friend? I wondered. *No one knows I'm here. I didn't call anyone.* But I silently followed his lead down a hallway, then into the lobby and over to a desk near the exit.

The officer behind the desk nodded toward a man standing off to the side. "He paid the two hundred to bail you out," he said. "You're free to go."

"But I don't know him," I said, confused.

The casually dressed stranger smiled gently and came over to me. He was tall, with dark hair and a muscular build. I guessed he was in his fifties.

"I'm Danny," he said. "I'm a friend of Glen's. He asked me to come get you."

At the mention of Glen's name, I felt a wave of relief. Glen was my boss at Doria's. Still, this made no sense to me. I hadn't called him. How did he know I'd been arrested?

"Let's get you out of this place."

Though Danny was a stranger, his face looked kind and his voice was gentle. I decided I'd ask my questions later. Glen must have heard what had happened to me across from the restaurant and sent this guy to get me. Right then, all I knew was that this kind-looking stranger was a way out of the frightening police station.

It was very dark outside. *I must have been in there for hours,* I thought.

As Danny led me to his car, he said, "You must be hungry and thirsty. I live close by. Let's stop by my place and get you some food and something to drink. Then I'll take you home."

I trusted him and followed along. He opened the front passenger car door for me.

"How did Glen know what happened?" I asked once we pulled away from the station.

"I don't know," Danny said. "But he called me and asked me to come get you."

Only minutes later, we were driving through a well-kept suburban neighborhood. Then we pulled into the driveway of a large, attractive home. I noticed the landscaping was well manicured, and there were decorative black bars on the windows and the front door. I followed him to the door, and like a true gentleman, he opened it and stepped aside, allowing me to step in first. The living room lights were on, and the place was neat and beautifully furnished.

"Let's go to the kitchen and rustle up some food."

First he got me a glass of water. I realized I was parched and gulped it down, then took a seat at the kitchen table as he got out a plate and some silverware.

That's when the room started to swirl a little. At first I assumed the funny feeling was the lingering effect of shock from being arrested and locked up. Danny turned and studied me for a moment, then said something, but I couldn't make out his words. His voice sounded muffled and far away. Everything looked blurry. Suddenly, panic swept over me as I realized he must have put something in my glass of water. I quickly stood but almost lost my balance, and I sank back into the chair with a jolt.

He grabbed my arm, and the next thing I knew I was being pulled down a hallway and into a bedroom. I wanted to resist, but I was too drugged. I was incredibly weak and dazed. Danny shoved me, knocking me onto the bed. Then he threw himself on top of me.

The sickening familiarity of being raped again overwhelmed me. I actually found myself grateful for whatever drug Danny had slipped into my glass of water, because somewhere amid the pain and disgust and horror, I slipped into unconsciousness.

When I awoke, the room was dark. I was alone, sprawled across the bed, and my black work slacks and panties were off. I sat up and saw them crumpled on the floor. I grabbed them and quickly pulled them on.

Faint moonlight shone through the window shade, and I scanned the room, then lunged for the door and tried the doorknob. Locked. I rushed over to the window and pulled up the shade. There, on the other side of the glass, were the black bars I'd naively assumed were just for decoration. For the second time that night, I was trapped behind bars.

How can this be happening? What's going on? This nightmare can't be real.

The evening's events flashed through my mind like a movie in fast-forward. Mere hours ago, I was leaving work after a typical shift. These bizarre events were inconceivable. I wanted to scream, to break the glass and rattle the bars to see if they'd give way so I could escape. I looked back at the door, wondering if I could throw myself against it hard enough to break out.

But I dared not make a sound. I was afraid that if I made any noise, my captor would come back and brutalize me again. I was trembling, fearing what else he was going to do with me. I turned back to face the window, and though bright moonlight shone on my face, a dark dread poured into my soul. *What happens next? What else will I have to endure?*

And with that fear came the most devastating and hopeless realization of the entire nightmare: All this felt very familiar. It was something I'd known since childhood. The circumstances were different, but the impact would be the same.

Once more I clearly recognized the powerlessness of being victimized, of being overpowered, trapped, and beaten. Of feeling hopeless. All those painful, bitter experiences had taught me that I had only one option: silence. Any other choice would multiply my suffering and pain.

So I chose silence.

Part 3

GROOMED
TO BE A VICTIM

1960–1972

5

THROUGH THE EYES
OF A CHILD

When I was a child, I spoke like a child,
I thought like a child, I reasoned like a child.

1 CORINTHIANS 13:11

I HELD MY BREATH, straining to hear any sounds of Mom and Dad coming from the hallway or the living room downstairs. Silence. Lifting my blanket carefully, I slid my feet into my slippers and tiptoed over to press my ear against the closed door. Still not a sound. I was nervous but pretty certain the coast was clear.

I glanced at my bedside alarm clock. It was 2:13 a.m. Surely Mom and Dad would be asleep by now, even though it was Christmas Eve. They'd stayed up late rustling around in the living room, arranging gifts under the tree, but I'd heard them come upstairs to their bedroom some time ago.

My door squeaked a little as I pulled it open just wide enough to stick my head into the hallway. The other four bedroom doors were all closed, with no lights peeking out from under them. All was still, convincing me that my two brothers and two sisters were asleep. Not wanting the squeaking of my door to wake anyone, I squeezed into the hallway without opening it any farther. Although the thumping of my heart sounded loud enough to wake the whole house, I pressed forward, creeping past my oldest sister's closed bedroom door and keeping my eyes on Mom and Dad's room. Then I tiptoed toward the stairs and down toward the living room. I paused halfway, just as the living room came into full view.

The faint glimmer from the streetlight filtered through the window sheers, casting strange shadows. I drew a quick breath as I saw all the gifts sprawling under the tree, across the room, and around the television. Even though, as a seven-year-old and the youngest of five, I knew that Santa wasn't real—my older siblings had long since burst my bubble about him and the Easter Bunny—it was still a magical scene. Every memory I had of Christmas morning was that there were more gifts than I could count. It seemed this year—1960—would be no exception.

However, every year had also brought distinct disappointment. So this year I was determined to take matters into my own hands to avoid that familiar pain. I'd made a plan. Now was my opportunity. Could I pull it off?

I crossed the living room to the Christmas tree. Where to start? So many gift tags to check, but I made quick work of scanning for my middle sister's name in Mom's familiar handwriting. Every Christmas, I'd watched with envy as my sister opened her gifts. Without fail, her gifts always seemed better than mine. We might both get a doll, but hers always had the prettier hair or the more awesome outfit. We always each got a sweater or two, but hers were always *my* favorite color. She was two years older than me, but still about my size.

This year, I'm getting the prettiest stuff, I thought. I was going to make sure of it.

It took only a few minutes to identify five or six of her gifts that looked promising. My fingers tingling with excitement, I picked up the first one. Ever so gently I peeled back the Scotch tape on a corner or two, slid the box partway out, and peered inside. Yes! Such a beautiful purple. Now to find a package with my name of similar size and feel. Once found, I peeled back its wrapping and saw a sweater for me. Brown. Ugh. Ever so gently I peeled off both name tags and switched them. Then on to the next box.

What will Mom think when I open these gifts in the morning? I was hoping that if she noticed, amid the craziness of five kids tearing packages open, she'd just figure she got the packages mixed up and mislabeled them.

All went smoothly. I kept my eye on the elegant grandfather clock, and within fifteen minutes I'd swapped tags on three gifts—the purple sweater, the doll with the long blond hair, and a pair of boots. I was satisfied. Making sure I'd placed each package back in its original spot, I took one last look over the room to make sure nothing was out of place, then tiptoed back up the stairs, snuck into my room, and slid into bed. My plan had worked! I quivered with excitement as I tried to calm down and get back to sleep.

They may all call me stupid, I thought, *but I can outsmart them.* I fell asleep thinking of brushing the long blond hair on my new doll. She was just what I wanted, and now she'd be mine.

Christmas morning was perfect. I'd never had a better one. We got through all the gift opening with no fighting or shouting—a miracle in itself—and I weathered Mom's confused looks without spilling the beans. As the family gathered noisily around her spectacular Christmas dinner that afternoon, I was wearing my new purple sweater and a bright smile. My secret was safe.

Little did I know that keeping secrets would become a life skill that had the power not only to protect me but to hold me captive as well.

•   •   •

Looking back on that Christmas morning, I understand what a sad scene it was. At the tender age of seven, I'd felt that something was so broken in my family that I had to take matters into my own hands or suffer the familiar disappointment that an older sibling's happiness seemed more important than my own.

Sadly, something *was* broken in my family, but from my earliest memories, the message I received was that the broken something was *me*. According to my family members, I was stupid. According to my mother, I *sounded* stupid when I talked. And Dad? While I don't recall him placing such explicit labels on me, I definitely got the sense that he saw me as slower than normal. Besides, I can't forget the feeling of his mighty hand smacking me so hard that I'd go flying across the room. That definitely sent the message that there was something wrong with me.

"You didn't start talking until you were five," I was told more than once. And that was true. To this day, I don't know why. Was it trauma? A developmental challenge? A learning disability? I suspect all were true.

Looking back, it's clear that I suffered from a serious learning disability of some kind, but it was never diagnosed or addressed or treated in any way. I couldn't articulate my thoughts. I couldn't study. I couldn't process information effectively. Even when I was held back a year in elementary school, I struggled. Sadly, because my issues were left unidentified and untreated, I was vulnerable.

I believed what others said about me—as children do. I was *not enough*. I was *a disappointment*. I was *broken*. And I couldn't be fixed. I wet the bed, which humiliated me, but I seemed unable to put an end to it. I bit my nails right down to the skin, sometimes till they bled, but I couldn't stop no matter how often I was scolded for it. Mom tried to help by putting a foul-tasting orange iodine polish on them. It burned my fingers, my lips, and my tongue, but I'd just grimace and keep on biting my nails. To top it off, I was a little large for my age—taller than most of my classmates. I was about the same size as my middle sister, who was two years older. My size in comparison to my classmates made me feel awkward. Embarrassment and shame were my constant companions. I felt like I didn't fit in anywhere.

Like other family members before me, I attended St. Anthony's, a Catholic school for students in kindergarten through eighth grade. One day in first grade, as the teacher was speaking to the class, I raised my hand for permission to go to the restroom.

"Put your hand down, Gina," I was told. I complied as I always did. But the urge got stronger. I raised my hand again. At first the teacher ignored me. Then she turned to me and again told me to lower my hand.

"I need to go the bathroom," I announced.

"Gina, you're just trying to get attention. Now keep your hand down."

Her words reminded me of what my mother often said to me: "You're just trying to get attention." So, obediently, I kept my hand down and tried to control the urge, but unsuccessfully. Moments later, my seat felt wet, and then a puddle began growing under my chair. I was aghast. Unfortunately, I wasn't the only one who saw it. Snickers began around me, and soon the entire class was pointing and laughing. I felt my face glowing red with embarrassment, and I was so humiliated I just wanted to disappear. I carried the shame of being "the girl who wet her pants" for the rest of that school year.

Were my mother and teacher right? Was I always seeking attention? I didn't think so. But looking back, I know I craved the affection that always seemed to elude me. Sadly, I learned at a young age that winning attention and winning affection could produce vastly different experiences.

One evening, Mom served peas with dinner. I hated peas. I

always had. (I still do!) Rather than force them down, I had the clever idea of secretly feeding them to Dino, our french poodle. Unfortunately, I wasn't as effective at being secretive as I'd hoped, and Mom discovered the truth. She was angry and pushed herself back from the table to come after me. Afraid I was about to get hit, I scrambled out of my chair and ran.

Mom jumped up and cut me off from my planned escape route, and I found myself trapped in the corner of the dining room. Then she reached over to the table and grabbed the pitcher of red Kool-Aid. I couldn't imagine why—until she held the pitcher over my head and began pouring. I screamed in protest as the ice-cold liquid flowed over my face, down my neck and torso, and finally onto my brand-new white Keds. I watched my treasured sneakers turn pink to the soundtrack of my entire family laughing uproariously. Well, I wasn't laughing with them. I was humiliated.

I can't help but wonder if that incident gave me the idea of using humor to my advantage. At times I compensated for the lack of positive attention the only way I knew how—through acting silly. If classmates and siblings—or even my own mother—were going to laugh at me anyway, I'd try to win their laughter in creative ways. I'd try to be entertaining. Unfortunately, others often found me irritating rather than entertaining, and I'd just get in more trouble. Not only was I seen as stupid; I was trouble. I was a problem. I was the black sheep.

I longed for words of praise and affirmation from anyone—family, teachers, friends—but they didn't come. I craved a sense of inclusion and belonging. Unfortunately, this set me up as an easy mark for my mischievous and sometimes downright devious family members. After all, it seems that most kids are naturally wired to take advantage of younger, weaker kids. I, on the other hand, was trusting and gullible—naturally wired to be manipulated.

"Gina, would you like me to take you for ice cream?" one family member asked.

I eagerly said yes.

"Okay, but first you have to go very quietly into your mom's room. She has a tin can in her closet on the floor that has beautiful coins in it. Go bring me a few. And don't say anything to anyone!"

Off I'd go on the secret errand, clueless that I was stealing the precious Krugerrands (gold coins from South Africa) that my grandfather had left to my mother.

"Gina, would you like me to take you shopping?"

"Oh, yes!" I'd answer.

"Your dad carries some loose change in his pants pockets that he doesn't need. Bring me some. But don't tell! It's a secret. Then we'll go shopping."

Once again, I'd run off and do so without any realization that I was being used. It never occurred to me that I was doing anything wrong. I just thought I was doing some favors. I was desperate for attention and acceptance, so I leaped at such opportunities.

One night one of my family members said, "Mommy wants me to cut your hair."

I loved having older girls around and always wanted to hang out with them and play with their makeup and hair. They, however, weren't interested in hanging out with me. Now this family member wanted to cut my hair? I was all for it! Compliant and trusting, I sat on the side of the bed, legs dangling, as I watched clumps of my long, wavy, thick, beautiful, dark-brown hair falling around me. When the act was done, I went to back to sleep, assuming all was well.

The next morning, when Mom came to wake me, she screeched, "What happened to your hair?"

All that was left were short, wild spikes pointing in all directions, making me all the more the laughingstock of the kids at school and in the neighborhood. The humiliation felt unbearable, yet I had no choice but to bear it. But far harder to bear was my sister's betrayal.

An older family member offered to fix my hair, and my mom agreed. That meant cutting some parts even shorter to even it out. In the end I wore a hat and tried to hide the little hair I had left.

Of course, if these examples were as dark as it got in my family, I wouldn't be calling my home broken at all. I knew kids could be mean to each other. Sadly, this was just the tip of the iceberg.

. . .

One day the sound of angry voices downstairs in the living room shattered my peaceful play in my bedroom. I'd been brushing the long, blond hair of my doll, but I dropped her in an instant and ran to the stairs to see what was going on. It was Dad again, this time fists clenched, closing the short distance between himself and another one of my family members. I knew this wouldn't end well. I'd witnessed enough knock-down, drag-out fights in my home to know that they almost always escalated until someone was on the floor, hurt.

For a moment, they stood head-to-head. One of them screamed something I didn't understand. Dad took a step back and looked ready to swing, when suddenly I saw my mother rush in from the kitchen.

"Stop!" she screamed. "Enough!" She was running fast and, in an instant, threw herself between them. But she wasn't fast enough. Dad's swing was already in motion. I could tell he tried to pull back, but too late. Mom went flying and landed crumpled on the floor.

Next it seemed like everything happened at once.

"No! Mary! I didn't mean to. I didn't see you. Are you all right?" Dad was kneeling by her motionless body.

I couldn't breathe.

Then Mom groaned. I'd never been so relieved in my life to hear a sound. I barreled down the stairs and threw myself over her, sobbing. Whatever transpired next is lost in the fog of old memories. Mom recovered from the incident with no visible injuries, though I can't speak for her emotional pain. But I can speak for mine. I was traumatized. Again. It wouldn't be the last time Mom went to the floor trying to stop fights.

I didn't know the terms *domestic violence* or *dysfunctional family*, but I lived with the consequences of both throughout my childhood. Ours was a volatile family—a loud, emotional, arguing, fighting family. Father against child, brother against brother, brother against sister—and it seemed to me that everyone was against *me*. Sometimes, as I watched the violence taking place, I was so worried that someone would get seriously hurt that I snuck to the phone and called the police, then hid in the coat closet until they'd come and gone.

"Who called the police?" someone inevitably asked afterward. I never confessed. My family probably assumed it was some neighbor who'd heard the fighting from across the street or walking by our front yard. The police would come and talk to my parents. Everyone calmed down, and I was always relieved I'd called. It was the only thing I knew I could do that would make a difference.

I desperately wanted the violence to end. The physical effects of witnessing the family I loved abusing one another were just as painful as the emotional impact. My stomach would get tied in knots. My heart would race. I'd quiver and shake for a long time after each episode. It frightened me to no end.

For several years of my childhood, I felt that the worst thing I suffered was witnessing physical violence. Then something even worse happened.

• • •

I confess it would be far easier to describe some difficult events if I clearly spelled out the identities of those involved and provided more details, but frankly, that wouldn't be wise. Most of those

I'm writing about are still alive. I have no desire to expose these individuals for deeds done many years ago, nor do I want to stir up animosity, anger, or resentment. The truth is, the *who* doesn't matter anymore. (These days, thanks to much counseling and healing, I have no ax to grind and no record to set straight.)

So I've coined a term for a small group of individuals in my life who, over the years, inflicted much abuse and pain. (In fact, decades later, a few still try.) I will call them "the pack." In this book, *the pack* refers to a mix of people, male and female, of varying ages, whom my parents trusted, and whom I, too, should have been able to trust. They were in our inner circle, frequently in our home and at family events. They were insiders to our affairs. In fact, the name-calling I endured all my life—of being called "stupid" and "retarded" and "idiot" and "ugly" and so on—consistently came at me from the pack. No one stopped them, rebuked them, or even admonished them. I was fair game to them. They repeatedly hurt me in a variety of ways, physically and emotionally.

Even though the individuals in the pack will remain nameless throughout my story, I have a clear purpose in writing about the following events, as well as events later in my life: I want to help readers understand that children who are exposed to and victimized by abuse in any form come away with a broken view of normalcy, of family, of trust, of self, and of love. This process grooms them to become victims in the future, to see themselves as worthless and deserving of abuse, to live with shame and fear, to accept being mistreated, and to be unaware of how and when to set healthy boundaries. You'll see how I was groomed—how I was, in some twisted way, trained and coached to believe I had no value, no self-respect, and no dignity. I was convinced that I was worthless and that my very existence was a problem—a conviction that followed me into adulthood.

. . .

One day, when I was around eight years old, I was playing on the floor in my room. The house was fairly quiet. Mom was downstairs in the kitchen. I stood up to fetch a toy from my closet when suddenly I was aware of someone much larger approaching me from behind. I was about to turn when a hand reached around from behind and covered my mouth, hard. I tried to yell, but the hand was so firm I couldn't make more than a muffled sound in my throat. The next thing I knew I was being pushed onto my bed, on my back, and now I could see him. It was someone we knew. Someone I was supposed to trust. A member of the pack.

The free hand of my assailant groped my entire body, starting at the neck and roughly working its way down. At first, I fought to get away by struggling and writhing, but I was helpless. His strength far outmatched mine, and he pressed his body against me, pinning me to the bed. Again, I tried to scream, but his hand stifled the sound. He didn't say a word as he slid his hand everywhere under my clothing, touching every part of my body. I didn't have words for what he was doing to me, but I felt sick to my stomach and horrified. Finally he stopped groping me and whispered in my ear, "You'd better not tell anyone. I'll tell them you're lying, and they'll never believe you." Then he lifted his weight off me, allowing me to roll out from under him and jump up.

Instantly I ran out my door, down the stairs, and burst into the kitchen. I could tell he was following me, but at an easy pace. Mom, startled, looked first at me, then at him as he strolled into the kitchen.

"Mom, he pushed me down on my bed and . . . and . . ." I was at a loss for words. My mother looked at me quizzically. "He touched me where he shouldn't have!"

"Good grief. There Gina goes again," he said, as if surprised by my story. "Making up wild stories to get attention. Why does she do that?" He chuckled and shrugged.

"Gina, Gina," Mom said. "What am I going to do with you?"

She shook her head, then turned her attention back to the vegetables she was cutting.

I stood wide-eyed and speechless. Stunned. *She doesn't believe me!* I thought. She took his word for it without asking him a single question? Why? How could this be? Did this person have some power over my own mother? Was she afraid of what might happen if she dared to believe me instead of him?

"But Mom," I started to protest, "I'm telling the truth."

She just waved her hand dismissively in response. Case closed.

She'd clearly made up her mind, and I knew better than to push. Silence was my only option. I don't recall what I did next. Whatever it was, I know I did it in defeat. But I do remember what I felt in that moment, even though I didn't have the vocabulary to put it into words back then. I felt dirty. Soiled. Powerless. Beaten. Hopeless. And I felt twice violated—first physically and emotionally by my assailant and then by my mother, whom I'd expected to be my protector.

Somehow he'd gotten away with it. He was skipping away scot-free while I was deeply wounded and labeled as the guilty one. My blood boiled at the injustice of it, yet I was helpless to change the outcome. I was victimized. And I felt ashamed of how powerless I was. I was the violated one, yet I had to bear the blame on top of it. For supposedly lying to get attention.

Little did I know that this feeling would come storming back into my life again and again in the years to come. Though the circumstances, the assailants, and the degree of violation would vary, I would grow accustomed to being the victim—and become practiced at carrying the shame.

Years later, as I stood at that barred window in the attractive suburban house where Danny, the violent rapist, held me captive, this was the event that came rushing back to mind—along with the sickening emotions.

6

MIXED MESSAGES

"YOU KNOW, GINA, I was just sixteen when I came to America from Italy," Dad said early one Saturday morning as he drove the two of us to his shop. I already knew this. Dad had told me the story many times, but I loved hearing it, so I didn't interrupt.

"My parents came to America when I was thirteen, but they wanted to get established here before bringing over the rest of the family, so they took only my oldest brother. My middle brother and I had to stay in Italy and move in with my grandparents. My grandfather was a hard man. A good man and a hard worker, but very strict, with a mean temper."

Even at the tender age of eight, I wondered if he realized he was describing himself perfectly. Like his grandfather before him,

Dad had a temper that flared easily and often, and he ruled with an iron fist—literally.

"The older I got, the harsh beatings I had to take from him were more frequent," Dad continued. "It got so bad, I even ran away a few times, but somehow I always wound up back under his roof. Finally, when I was sixteen, my parents brought me here to America, to New Jersey. I didn't speak English but went to school anyway and just picked it up as I went. I also had to work hard to earn money, of course. I eventually became a barber. It took me a long time to work up to having a barbershop of my very own while also going to school to learn about gems and diamonds."

As Dad said this, he was unlocking the door of his two shops in one. One side was his barbershop, and on the other side, separated off by a partition, was his jewelry store. I followed him inside, and he let me turn on the overhead lights and turn off the alarm system.

"After many years, I had lots of loyal customers, and I made the time to get to know the jewelry business, too. There was lots to learn, Gina. This is why it's important to work hard in school."

Up to that point, I'd been content listening, proud of my dad for being a self-made man, but when I heard those final words, I cringed. I did work very hard in school, and I wanted to say so, but I was afraid I'd start an argument and ruin our time together. I liked this gentle Daddy. I didn't want angry Daddy to emerge.

The truth was, in school I tried everything I could think of to listen and learn what the nuns were teaching us. But I struggled. It always seemed like everyone except me understood the lessons. I just didn't get it. I fumbled over words when I tried to read. I didn't understand what to do with all the numbers in math. They just didn't make sense to me. I got a knot in my stomach as I thought back to my last report card. On the left side, next to the subjects, was a list of Fs, with maybe a couple of Ds. And on the right side, where the behavior chart was, most sections were marked with a U for "unsatisfactory." Thankfully, there were times when a few Ss (for "satisfactory") appeared, but they were seldom. To me, my report card was just proof that something wasn't right about me.

It didn't make it any easier that others in my family did well in school. "Didn't you know you were left on our doorstep?" they sometimes told me. "You aren't really part of our family at all."

Fortunately, Dad didn't bring up my report card that morning. He was checking the cash register. I followed as he led the way to the door on the side wall, and we stepped through to his jewelry store.

I loved being with Dad in this special place. So many beautiful rings and necklaces and bracelets with colorful stones. He kept the glass display cases sparkling clean, and I knew never to touch them so I wouldn't leave fingerprints.

"Gina, the most important thing in running a business is to take good care of your customers. Always be respectful, polite, and appreciative. Most of my customers in the barbershop and jewelry store have been customers for many years. They come back again and again because they know they can trust me and I will treat them well." I knew he was telling the truth. When Dad was with his customers, he was incredibly patient and kind, and he made everyone feel special and appreciated.

I loved the precious times I got to spend with Dad at his businesses. I wished I could come every Saturday. I'd much rather be with Dad there than at home with my siblings. Usually on Saturday mornings I had to stay at home with them, where my oldest brother was in charge while Mom went to help Dad in the shops. But at the shops, everyone was always so kind and polite—including Dad and Mom. There was no arguing, no hitting, no name-calling, no threats of violence. Nobody ever lost their temper.

Why can't it be like this at home? I wondered. *I'm not afraid here like I am all the time at home.*

Some days I played quietly in the back break room while Dad worked, but that morning, while daydreaming of when I'd be old enough to work in the store with him, I was cleaning his display cases with glass cleaner, as I'd seen him do countless times. Then I heard the tinkle of the bell from the front door of the jewelry store.

"Excuse me, Marty," Dad said to the man in the barber chair, "but do you mind if I check with my customer next door?"

"No problem, Tom," the man said.

Dad then took off his barbering smock and crossed through the inside door to the jewelry store. After several minutes, he was back with a thank-you to his customer for waiting. I was very proud of how well Dad treated his customers.

When lunchtime came, Dad would take me across the street to the deli and order my favorite meal: a bologna sandwich. They knew him at the deli and always greeted him warmly, talking happily as they made our lunch. I felt important just being at his side.

On the occasions I watched Mom helping out in the shops, I was proud of her, too. She had a big, beautiful smile and was very warm and welcoming to customers. She seemed happy there, and I wondered why I couldn't make her as happy at home as the customers made her.

Mom didn't tell me stories of when she was little like Dad did. But I did know that she must have loved her own mother very much. I'd been told that when Mom was expecting me, her mother died suddenly of a cerebral hemorrhage. Poor Mom was so heartbroken that she had what Dad described as a nervous breakdown before I was born. It took her a long time to get better, so she couldn't take care of me as a newborn and needed help from other people. I sometimes wondered if that was why it seemed she was closer to my sisters than to me. Though I know she loved me the best she could, I always feared that I was a disappointment to her. I seemed to embarrass her, especially if I talked in front of her friends. I longed for her to look at me with pride in her eyes—a longing that went unsatisfied.

Unlike Dad, Mom was an only child and was born in America, but her father came over from northern Italy, so she, like Dad, was raised in an Italian family. Italian food, Italian traditions, Italian accents. Mom was the ultimate homemaker who loved cooking for her family. One expression of her love for us was that every Sunday afternoon she would gather us all at the table to enjoy the fabulous dinner she had lovingly created for us. And oddly enough, in spite of the arguments, the fights, or the violence we had inflicted on one another, we shared the meal as if we were one big, happy family. Mom also enjoyed making our home beautiful each season of the year, and when she prepared a holiday meal, the table was a feast for the eyes as much as for the stomach, overflowing with an abundance of food spread out in lovely dishes and bowls.

In my preschool days, my special times with Mom were on Fridays, when she'd take me grocery shopping with her. She was always careful picking out the perfect cuts of meat and the most beautiful fruits and vegetables. We'd go shopping in the morning and then have lunch out at a deli or restaurant. It seemed to me that everyone knew Mom, just like they knew Dad.

Mom sometimes sang songs to me. I loved the sound of her voice and would cuddle up close to her. But perhaps my favorite times with her were when we went to the beach together. We'd sit under our big, striped umbrella, her in her beach chair and me playing in the sand. Having Mom all to myself was a special treat because she was often helping Dad with his businesses, and I'd be left at home with my siblings in charge. When at home, she was busy around the kitchen or cleaning house or interacting with my siblings. It wasn't easy for her to respond to the different needs of her children, and often I felt like I was invisible to her.

I never doubted that Mom and Dad loved me, as they loved my brothers and sisters, but I often felt they didn't approve of me very much. Yet if I measured love by gift giving, I was well loved. As I mentioned before, I was often envious of the gifts my siblings received, believing that my parents thought of me as less important. But the truth is that they showered all of us with gifts every year at Christmas. Back-to-school season brought shopping trips for new clothes, as did Easter Sunday and the arrival of spring. Summer meant a new swimsuit and the arrival of my birthday in June. Mom made a point each year of planning wonderful birthday parties for us kids. And she always made holidays special for the entire family.

Apart from gift-giving occasions, my most memorable moments of feeling my parents' love and care for me were when I was one-on-one with either of them. Sadly, those times were the exception rather than the rule. On a daily basis, I was the youngest, quietest, most easily overlooked kid in a noisy, rowdy family. Most of the time, I felt ashamed at best, abused at worst, and afraid almost always. I felt afraid even when I wasn't the object of derision, as if I was always waiting for the other shoe to drop. Seems I never had to wait long.

One Saturday morning while my parents were at Dad's shops, I was home with some other family members. They were hanging out in the living room when one of my sisters came through the room. She was wearing a pretty yellow dress—the kind that had crinoline sewn into the skirt so that it flared out. One of the guys gave her an order, and she responded flippantly. He didn't tolerate that, so he lunged at her. She screamed as he turned her upside down, held her by her ankles, and dangled her in the air. Her beautiful yellow dress now flopped open, exposing her panties for all to see. He then started to spank her bottom. The more she screamed, the harder he smacked her.

I stood speechless, a witness to the indignity thrust upon my sister. I wanted to scream with her, to demand she be put down, to pummel the victimizer with my fists for inflicting such humiliation. But I did nothing. I said nothing. I stood by, embarrassed on my sister's behalf, my heart breaking for her. I dared not do or say anything for fear that I would be his next victim. I was all too conscious of how often I'd been the object of the pack's amusement. More times than I could count, I'd been grabbed and had my lips roughly and painfully stretched out or my sides and arms pinched while I was called fat. I'd feel my victimizers' eyes all over me, their faces contorted in smirks at my expense. I was powerless to do anything but wait for the moment they'd release me, or I'd writhe and wriggle my way free, then run from the room, the sounds of their rude laughter echoing in my ears.

It was pointless to run to my mother upon her return with reports of being victimized. As far as I could tell at the time, abusers never suffered consequences for their abuse. Incidents like this made me feel like I was fair game for whatever cruelty could be inflicted outside the scope of my parents' vision.

One Saturday while I was home and my parents were working, one of my abusers got angry at me for some reason. As I recall, it had something to do with me not making him breakfast quickly enough. He started to chase me, and fearing a beating, I ran from him as fast as I could through the house. I took shelter in the first-floor bathroom and locked the door, which had a thick frosted-glass window in it. He was coming after me so fast that when he reached the door, he pushed it hard and broke right through the glass. I was cowering on the floor behind the toilet and suddenly had shards of glass falling all over me. A sharp piece cut my thumb. Blood was soon flowing, and I was in tears. My next memory is of sitting in the emergency room with my mother by my side as I got stitches. Apparently, she'd come home soon after the incident to take me to the hospital.

"Why did he hurt me? Why did he do that?" I asked her.

"He didn't mean to do that. He loves you," she said. "He loves you very much. He did that because he loves you."

At the time, I didn't know what my mother was trying to say. It certainly didn't feel like love. But her words stuck with me: *He did that because he loves you.* As twisted as that reasoning may sound, those words were consistent with what I'd been witnessing and experiencing in my home for as long as I could remember. Dad— who loved his family—beating my brothers and sisters, and me as well. My family members inflicting pain and humiliation on each other. My mother seemingly averting her eyes from the brutality in her home—living with it, adapting and adjusting to it and, in essence, tolerating it. The message I got was this: *Being loved means being hurt.* If an abuser hurts you physically, that means you are loved. Love and abuse go hand in hand. Abuse *is* love. And protecting the one who hurt you is love as well.

Sadly, it was a message I internalized. A message that would carry a hefty price tag for years to come.

• • •

"The priest just called," Mom shouted from the bottom of the stairs. "He'll be here in about half an hour. I want everyone's room picked up now."

This wasn't a surprise visit. Mom must have called him that morning, as she frequently did the morning after a violent fight in our home. Just as I often called the police when fighting broke out in our home, Mom and Dad often called the priest the next day, asking that he come and bless all the rooms of our home. Within an hour of their phone call, the priest arrived, dressed in black from head to toe, except for his white collar. Priests always scared me a little bit. They seemed so somber, so serious.

I recognized him, of course, not only from Sunday-morning Mass every week but also from school at St. Anthony's. The school was attached to our church building, where we attended faithfully. Familiar or not, I felt afraid around him, and I hung back when he arrived.

First, he and Mom went into the dining room, where there had been a fistfight the night before. They spoke quietly to each other, then came into the living room, where I was sitting on the sofa. The priest bowed his head and was very quiet and still for a few moments. I knew he was praying, but I wondered exactly what he was saying to God. And I wondered if he could hear God talking back to him. Then, without a word, he headed for the stairs. Mom followed. They went from bedroom to bedroom, following the same routine. He'd bow his head at the door of each room, making the sign of the cross and splashing holy water on the doors. He'd stand very still for a few moments and then move on to the next room. When he'd been through the whole house, Mom walked him outside, and he drove off.

The following Sunday in church, after the service, I watched this priest as he shook hands with people in the aisle. Did he go to the homes of all the other people, too, after they had big fights? I just assumed everyone had fights like ours. It was my normal.

There was also an occasion that brought the priest to our home annually, and that was when my mother prepared a "Saint Joseph's table"—a tradition many Italian Catholics celebrate. In the Italian Catholic tradition, Joseph, the husband of Mary and the legal earthly father of Jesus, is the patron saint of fathers, immigrants, craftspeople, and unborn children, among many others. March 19 is the Feast of Saint Joseph, or Saint Joseph's Day. According to a

Catholic tradition dating back to the Middle Ages, there was once a severe famine in Sicily. The peasants prayed to Saint Joseph for deliverance, and when the rains finally came, they held a grand celebration in his honor during which they filled tables with elaborate displays of food—especially beautiful decorative breads. This celebration became an annual event.

Some Catholic parishes celebrate with Saint Joseph's tables at the church building, while others may have parishioners host such displays in their homes. My mother, ever the gracious hostess, loved creating a stunning Saint Joseph's table in our home. She'd spend days preparing special recipes and baking breads in elaborate designs, then lovingly arrange them in a stunning display on our dining-room table. I loved watching it come together. Once all the food was prepared and on display, we would dress in our Sunday best, and the priest would come to bless the food before anyone was allowed to eat it. On this occasion, I wasn't at all afraid of the priest. He always had a smile on his face and complimented Mom, who beamed.

As a child, I understood that the church and the priest were very important to my parents, but I never really understood why. To me, church, like the priest, was always a little bit scary. I believed there was a God because I was told there was, but I associated Him with scary priests; strict, demanding, and seemingly ever-disapproving nuns at school; and long, boring services I didn't understand but was required to attend. In fact, as I understood it, even Mom and Dad were required to attend, but I was never quite sure who made that requirement. Was it God?

A very important book, the Bible, was kept in the front of the church on the altar. Only the priest read out of it, and altar boys turned the pages. I understood that God gave us lots of rules to follow, and there were certain prayers, like the Lord's Prayer, that we had to memorize. Our church and all its traditions were meaningless rituals to me. However, I truly believed that if I ever stepped into a different church, I would be struck by lightning.

But when I took my first Communion at the age of seven, I experienced something I'd never felt before. During the service, we were to speak these words: "Lord, I am not worthy to receive You, but just say the word and I shall be healed." Every time I spoke those precious words, I felt something very personal and intimate. I understood what it meant to not feel worthy, since that was a feeling I lived with all the time. But the thought that God could simply say the word and I'd be "healed" was a beautiful thought to me. I can't say I understood that thought, but it captured my heart and warmed it. And so I loved taking Holy Communion.

Just as I loved my father and felt close to him when he took me to his work, even though at other times I was terribly afraid of him.

Just as I loved my mother and felt close to her when she sang to me or took me grocery shopping, even though at other times I felt invisible to her.

Just as I loved my family and felt close to them when we all gathered around Saint Joseph's table, even though I lived in fear that they would hurt me.

And my abusers in particular? I can't say I loved them, but it seemed the rest of my family did. After all, they were treated like family.

Love, I discovered as a child, was very confusing, whether it was love for God or parents or siblings. It was filled with mixed messages. And so love always brought anxiety with it. Nail-biting, bed-wetting, hand-wringing, heart-pounding anxiety and fear on a near-daily basis. Blended with my feelings of shame and worthlessness, the thought of love left me feeling isolated and alone rather than connected. That was hard enough as a child, especially when coupled with learning disabilities that made comprehension and self-expression a challenge for me.

But as I would discover when I hit puberty, adding surging hormones, a drive for independence, and a hunger for affirmation into that complex mix of fear, loneliness, shame, longings, isolation, and confusing thoughts and feelings could be toxic and dangerous.

7

TRYING TO FLY

I APPROACHED SISTER MARY MARGARET one Friday afternoon as our ninth-grade class was lining up to go to confession.

"Sister, I don't think I need to go to confession this week. I have nothing to confess."

"Gina, everybody has to go to confession," she said matter-of-factly. "Every Friday. Now get in line."

I did as I was told and dutifully lined up, but I wasn't happy about it. My adjustment to Catholic high school wasn't going all that well. Just as I'd struggled from kindergarten through eighth grade, I continued to wrestle with learning every day of the week. In class after class, no matter how much effort I poured into listening, studying my textbooks, and trying to complete my homework, I came up short. I felt like a failure. I was embarrassed, ashamed, and frustrated. And now I was being told I had to confess my sins even when I couldn't think of any. Was I even a failure at confession? (Obviously, my understanding of sin was quite shallow. I thought of it as rule breaking, and I'd been conscientious about not breaking any rules that week.)

But I was determined I would not show up in the confession booth with nothing to say. In desperation, I tore a piece of paper from my notebook, and right there in line, leaning on my notebook, I began writing a list of sins. Not *actual* sins I'd committed but sins the priest would believe. Likely sins. I listed things like swearing and copying someone's homework and arguing with my mother and fighting with my sisters. I wrote them down so that in my nervousness I wouldn't get all tongue-tied and forget them in the booth.

By the time I got to the front of the line, I thought I had a pretty good list. The girl ahead of me exited the booth and I entered, list in hand. I began reading my sins aloud to the priest. Suddenly I heard what sounded like the priest standing up and opening his door. My own door then abruptly opened, and there he stood, scowling at me. He reached over, snatched the list from my hand, and quickly scanned it.

"Come with me, Gina," he said sternly, and in the blink of an eye I was being escorted to the principal's office. I couldn't imagine why, but clearly I was in big trouble. What went wrong? Had he been able to tell from my voice that I was lying and that these weren't really my sins? I hoped not.

I wasn't kept in the dark for more than a few minutes. The priest explained to the principal that during my confession, he'd heard the rustling of paper and become suspicious. The principal quickly scanned my list and was just as upset by it. Then I got a firm talking to. Didn't I know that genuine confession was to come from the heart? That confession wasn't a joke but was to be taken seriously? Somehow, they considered writing my sins on paper a lack of sincerity. I was so stunned by it all, I couldn't think of a response, not even when the principal picked up the phone and called my mother, asking her to come in for a conference.

In the end I was suspended—yes, suspended! My poor grades and now my "shenanigans" of not taking confession seriously were seen as evidence that I wasn't applying myself in school. To top it off, they reported to my parents that I was often silly or humorous in classes, which, they asserted, was disrespectful. The entire incident reinforced my self-image as a failure, an embarrassment. I was trouble with a capital *T*. I was the black sheep. And true to form, my family painfully reinforced that message at home.

I couldn't deny that I liked to make people laugh. As I mentioned before, my efforts as a younger child to use humor to deflect derision and mistreatment had been my instinctual coping method for dealing with the frequent insults and mockery I endured so often at school and home. If people were going to laugh at me, why not be funny and inspire them to laugh *with* me? If there was one positive label I'd been given during my elementary days, it was *funny*. I'd even earned some student awards as "Funniest in the Class." Finally some affirmation! I reveled in it. So when I moved up to high school, I set out to earn that reputation again, and I succeeded. But I still tried to be a respectful student and never used humor at the cost of others, whether students or teachers. I was genuinely surprised and hurt that an accusation of being humorous was lodged against me as part of the justification for my suspension.

Though I was respectful in using humor, there was a certain amount of rebellion brewing in my spirit, especially when it came to what I considered inconsequential rules. We wore school uniforms—for girls, a skirt, blouse, and sweater. The rules for the length of our skirts were unbending. I wasn't defiantly leading a rebellion, marching into school with my hemline well above my knees only to be sent back home. Rather, I joined in with other girls. We'd go to the restroom and roll up our skirt waistlines, which hiked our hemlines just a bit. Then if we made it partway through the day without getting caught, we'd roll up our waistlines some more.

There were also rules about keeping our hair under control—never too high. My hair was thick and wavy and not easily controlled, in spite of my efforts to manage it. So even my hair "failed" at school.

The nuns, of course, were well aware of all the common tricks and kept their eyes open for violators. One day a nun put my head under a water fountain because my hair was too poofy. My classmates thought this was hilarious, but I was humiliated and wanted to just disappear. And more than once I was smacked with a ruler after being told to unroll my skirt waistline. If the purpose of such punishments was to force me into submission, I'm afraid they had the opposite effect. Rather than becoming compliant, I slowly grew sneakier and more deliberate in my attempts to get around the rules.

Looking back today, I can see how all the negative factors in my life were planting seeds of anger and a yearning to escape disapproval during my freshman year of high school. Two factors in particular fed my quietly simmering frustration. One was the constant criticism I received at home—especially from my mother. I loved her dearly and longed for her approval, but it seemed always beyond my reach. Often my mother would look at me and say, "What are you going to *do* with yourself? Look at you. Just do *something*." I'd look in the mirror and see my ordinary self staring back, bewildered and shamed, wondering what I could possibly do to "fix" my broken self.

Other times, Mom would look at me in disgust—like she wasn't proud of me. As far as I could perceive, Mom was never proud of me. She frequently told me that I was an embarrassment to her. As a result of such words from her, other family members, and some nuns, along with classmates who taunted me for poor grades or "stupid" questions in class, I felt overwhelmed with negativity, unacceptance, and criticism. It seemed as if I had no value. If I wasn't accepted and loved by my own family members—who were supposed to love me—where was I to turn? Obviously not to nuns or priests. My abusers? Never. What about my peers? Some had taunted me since kindergarten. Though I didn't see it at the time, using humor was my best attempt to win the approval of others. It was also a way to hide my pain and my gnawing fear of rejection, of never being enough.

●　　●　　●

My freshman year of high school—which I had hoped would mark a new beginning—was proving to be even more painful than my grade-school years, both at home and at school. I'd watched with envy as each of my older siblings passed into the fascinating world of teenagers. One by one they'd been given more freedom, spending more time out of the house with friends and being involved in sports and school activities. They all succeeded at school, at making friends, and at winning more privileges and freedoms. I'd hoped for the same, but with the shame of being suspended early in the year, and always in trouble for my failing grades, I found myself trapped in a cycle of disappointing everyone, including myself.

Envying one of my sisters made my plight all the more painful. Since she was incredibly smart, she got to attend an out-of-state, premier boarding school for girls. My parents were terribly proud of her. Trips to her school for special family functions were a huge deal. I envied the way my parents took so many pictures of her and her teachers and her friends from all over the world. She was given lovely clothes and lived in a beautiful dorm room with girls who seemed to be rich and elegant and have very important families. She was beautiful and knew how to wear her hair and makeup perfectly. Her school had fancy dances where the girls wore gorgeous gowns. What a fairy tale! Oh, how I wanted her life! But by the time I was a freshman, I knew that kind of life would never be mine. I was Gina. The broken girl. The stupid girl. Funny, yes. Thank goodness for that one bright spot! But a failure nevertheless.

As I was soon to learn, things could get worse.

One day a priest came to our catechism class to discuss relationships, especially boy-girl relationships. This was in no way a sex-education talk. (We'd never had one in school, and I'd never had such a conversation at home.) But he invited us all to ask questions, and he'd answer them. Given the topic, I saw this as my chance to ask a question that I'd greatly wondered about but had never felt free to ask. I raised my hand.

"Yes, Gina?" the priest said.

"I was wondering, can a girl get pregnant by kissing a boy?"

The class erupted in laughter. The nun who usually taught this class blanched. And the priest? He glowered at me. I knew instantly I'd made a huge mistake. The laughter and snickering lingered, and it occurred to me that maybe I was the only one in the room who didn't already know the answer to my question. Clearly there was a big secret about how girls got pregnant, and everyone in the class seemed to know but me.

I wanted to disappear. I wanted the floor to open up and swallow me. But I also wanted to know the answer to my question. I wanted to be in on the big secret. Yet I could tell by looking at the priest and the nun that not only were they not going to answer, but I was also in *really big* trouble.

"That's enough now," the priest said to regain control of the classroom. Then he immediately sent me to the principal's office, and my parents were called.

I sat trembling in the principal's office with my parents and listened in shock as we were told that I was no longer welcome at the school. "Her grades are so poor as it is," the principal said, "that even if we were to keep her in the school, she'd have to repeat the year. On top of that, we simply can't tolerate such inappropriate behavior to win the laughter of her classmates. We've done what we can for Gina. We believe she'd be a much better fit in a public school."

I didn't try to explain that I hadn't asked the question for laughs. I didn't know how a girl got pregnant and didn't know it was rude to ask. I just sat there silently until the meeting was over. My parents were silent too. It was obvious I had deeply embarrassed them. I left the school with them that day, never to return. They didn't yell at me or punish me. They simmered in silence and never brought it up again. Because it was so close to summer break, I'd have to wait until fall to be enrolled at the local public high school.

Perhaps the most troubling thing of all was that they never addressed my question. I still didn't know how a girl got pregnant. I didn't know what my period was all about. I didn't have a clue as to how the reproductive system worked. And I figured I was the only one in the entire school who didn't know. But one thing was for sure: I was never going to ask again.

• • •

I was much lonelier in public school. At least at Catholic school, I'd known many of my classmates for several years. I'd been surrounded by familiar faces, and for the most part, I knew what to expect. Now I was afraid of failing in front of new classmates. Learning was still a major struggle. I was friendly and talkative in my new school and, as always, used humor to try to connect with others. Silliness was my shield, a way to protect myself from being vulnerable.

I kept my secrets in public school as well. I didn't tell anyone that violence was a normal occurrence at my house. Who'd ever believe me anyway? My own mother hadn't believed me. Better to just remain silent, try to avoid him, and move on without creating a scene when it happened again—which it always did. This was evidently part of being a teenage girl.

I was clueless about how to set boundaries or enforce them, or protest inappropriate treatment. My no meant nothing. I had learned from my family's example that boys and men just do these kinds of things, and it was our job as girls to live with it. Saying something, protesting, or fighting back was not only wrong; it was also considered disrespectful.

* * *

When I turned sixteen, I set my sights on a goal: getting a job. I wanted to earn my own money and feel independent. I wanted a good excuse to get out of the house more often. Dad, however, was dead set against my working outside the house, other than helping out at his shops.

Mom, on the other hand, seemed to understand my desire and, without telling my dad, supported the idea. "Just don't tell your father," she insisted as I headed out the door for my first day on the job as a cashier at a nearby grocery store.

On day one I learned how to use the cash register. It came easily to me, probably because I'd so often rung up customers at my dad's shops. On day two I was told I had good customer-service skills.

I felt so proud and accomplished. I'd always admired the way my dad served his customers, and now I was emulating him with great success. On day three I was partway into my shift when I saw my dad enter the store. My stomach lurched. Dad was heading straight my way. My instincts told me to duck and hide, but I took a deep breath and held my ground.

Dad walked right to my cash register, stepped around the counter, and without saying a single word, took hold of my arm and firmly led me toward the store exit. I saw my coworkers and even customers looking on with bewildered expressions, and I thought I'd die of embarrassment. So I hung my head and stared at the tile floor as we left the building. I never went back.

I was heartbroken. Since grade school I'd been trying my wings, yearning to fly, and it seemed to me I was tangled in a net that held me back. Fear and shame and worthlessness, violence and disability and warped messages kept me earthbound, leaving me confused about life, love, and identity.

For the balance of my high school years, I squeaked by academically, and the school kept passing me on to the next grade. It seemed that no one on the faculty noticed or cared about me, which was fine by me. And at home, the fact was well established that I was an academic failure, so as long as I attended school and didn't get in trouble or expelled, all was status quo.

Status quo and the teenage years don't coexist well, however. The status quo keeps all things the same, while the teen years typically thrust us toward change and development and struggle. Ready or not, for good or bad, all three awaited me.

8

BROKEN WINGS

"THAT'S IT, GINA! I've had it with your attitude!"

Dad was yelling so loudly, I was sure people living on the next block could hear it. "You're grounded. Now go your room!"

Trembling, I stood toe to toe with him. I rarely dared to defy my father, not even at seventeen. By nature, I was a peacemaker and just wanted the conflict to go away. Whenever my dad's temper flared, I'd usually cower and back away. Or go to my room and sulk. But by this age my attitude of peacemaking was changing to one of defiance. This time I was certain I was being treated unfairly, and I was determined to defend myself. As my trembling grew in intensity, I could sense my dad's temper was about to boil over. I'd come home late the night before, and he was so furious he began smacking me. That night I did not want a repeat, so I turned and went up to my room.

The next morning, although I knew I was grounded, I asked my sister if I could borrow her car. Then after Dad left for church, I got in and drove away. My heart was pounding so violently, I thought my chest would explode, but there was no turning back. I was headed to the most comforting place I could think of—my grandmother's house. Dad's mother. Nona Marie.

Nona Marie was the safest person I knew at that time. She met me at the door after I rang her bell. I fell into her arms weeping. She calmly led me to the kitchen table, handed me a box of tissues, and waited for me to speak. Through tears, I told her what had happened with Dad. I don't know how much time passed, but after a little while, we were having a snack of graham crackers with milk. I was feeling better now, and she was gently reassuring me that she loved and treasured me. After I learned to drive, I'd come to Nona Marie's often. We were very close. She understood me, believed me, and always made me feel like I was the best thing in the world. No one else ever made me feel like that.

A bit later, with my agreement, she went to the phone and dialed my father.

"Yes, Tom. She's here with me," I heard her say to Dad. "Now, I want you to stop hurting her. It's not right and you know it. She needs to be safe in her own home, for goodness' sake!"

I'd moved to my grandma's side so I could hear Dad's voice. He was composed now. "Okay, Mom. Just send her home. I won't hit her."

"You promise me you won't touch her if she comes home?" she asked with a warning in her voice.

After hanging up, my grandmother said in a reassuring tone, "Go on home. He's not going to hit you."

So I made the ten-minute drive home. When I pulled up, I noticed people in the backyard and remembered that Mom and Dad had planned a barbecue for that afternoon. I parked my sister's car but then saw Dad coming toward me. I assured myself that I wasn't afraid to see him, since he'd promised Nona Marie that he wouldn't hurt me. Yet I still braced myself. I'd been conditioned to fear the unknown and be on the defensive when it came to Dad. Hoping he'd keep his word to my grandmother, I walked up to him quietly.

"Why did you go? I grounded you. You weren't supposed to go out," he said calmly.

The soft tone of his voice reassured me.

Still feeling safe, I said, "Yeah. Well, I went anyway."

Not smart.

I didn't see his hand coming until I felt the slap. I stumbled sideways, and my face hit the side of our house, which was stucco. Searing pain radiated from both cheeks—one side from his open-handed slap and the other from my collision with the wall. As I caught my balance, I saw his hand coming at my head again. *Bam!* He deliberately drove my head into the stucco a second time. Then *whap!* Another blow. I felt warm blood rolling down the side of my face. Black spots appeared in front of my eyes. My ears rang. Somehow I caught sight of our guests looking on. They were watching, but no one stepped forward to protest the beating or protect me. I felt caught in an eerie scene, and I couldn't believe this was really happening. I had no protection. As I crumpled to the ground, Dad turned and walked back to the barbecue as if nothing had happened.

This was my daddy, the man who was supposed to love me more than any other man on earth. Just the week before, he'd invited me to help him in the jewelry store, where I'd rung up purchases and called customers to inform them their merchandise had arrived. And not long before that, he'd taken me to the jewelry district on Canal Street in New York City, where he'd asked me to help him pick out new merchandise. He'd spoken sweet words about how proud he was of me for learning so much about his business. Now I sat on the concrete bleeding, too hurt and stunned to do anything but sit still for several minutes. Not a single person came to check on me or help me up.

When I finally stood, I used the back of my hand to wipe the still-trickling blood from the side of my head and face and then crept into the house, up the stairs, and into the bathroom. After cleaning myself up, I wobbled into my bedroom and curled up on my bed.

This was love in my family. Sometimes I'd find kindness, along with flickers of hope, anticipation, and even warmth, but I had learned to never forget about the possibility of violence after promises of safety.

Love, as I'd been learning for years, was erratic. Dangerous. Painful. Unpredictable. Though at times it was nurturing and filled with promise, at other times it was devious and crushing. Love was not discipline but punishment. Love was not safe. Love could not be trusted. Nevertheless, I had to accept these circumstances and simply live with them. Like I always had. And why not? I was worthless. I was trouble. I was a disappointment.

Surely I didn't deserve any better.

●　●　●

"Look at what I brought you!" one of my family members announced one day as he entered the house through the kitchen door.

Mom turned to see him holding up a few plump, red tomatoes.

"They're beautiful!" she said as she accepted them and gave him a hug.

"They're from my friend Andy, from his mother's garden. He said they have too many and are giving them away."

Mom went on and on gushing over the tomatoes and thanking

him as if he'd grown them himself. I couldn't think of a time my mother had ever gushed over a gift *I'd* given her—not even a hand-made gift.

What would it be like to have attention and gratitude like that from Mom? I thought. I wanted, just once, for Mom to make a huge deal out of something I gave her.

A few months later, I stopped at the grocery store to pick up a few items for Mom, and a thick, beautiful London broil caught my eye. It was a cold winter day, and I was wearing a long coat with deep pockets. On an impulse, I reached into the meat cooler, grabbed two packaged steaks, and shoved them hurriedly into my pocket. I stole the meat! I'd never done anything like that before, but I had a plan.

That evening while Mom worked late at the jewelry store, I prepared a full meal with the London broil as the main course. When she came home, I took her coat and ushered her into the dining room, where I'd set a beautiful table.

"Made something special for you tonight, Mom," I said. I disappeared into the kitchen for a moment and returned with a lovely plate of London broil, potatoes, and green vegetables, which I set on the table before her.

I stood expectantly while she eyed the plate. She gazed up at me, a confused look on her face.

"I don't remember having this steak in the freezer," she said.

"Well, I got it for you. I bought it," I lied. "And I fixed it just for you." Then I waited for a big response. She took a bite and then another.

But the anticipated response never came. No exclamation of delight or surprise. No gushing words of gratitude.

"It's good. Thank you," she simply said halfway through the meal. And that was that. My craving for affirmation and connection with my mother once again went unsatisfied.

Gestures and gifts from me to Mom simply didn't work the way they worked for others. What would it take for my mother to throw her arms around me and say, "Wow! I love you so much! You know what? You don't need to do anything to earn my love. I simply couldn't love you more!"

When would I learn? Time and again I'd find myself trying hard and then harder, but for all the wrong reasons. Whatever I was doing, I did to get approval. To the point of insanity.

After Mom left the table, I cleared the dishes, thinking, *Enough will never be enough. I'll never be enough.*

• • •

I was craving safety, affirmation, connection, intimacy, and acceptance—all things I couldn't find at home. I was a lonely girl who felt isolated and angry and starved to be acknowledged, to be validated. I craved the feeling of being wanted. It was the perfect setup for what came next.

I met a guy I'll call John, who was a police officer. He was several years older, with an air of maturity and self-confidence. And yes, he noticed me all right. He told me I was beautiful and funny and irresistible.

No one had ever spoken such words to me before. Never! And he wanted to take me out. Like out of the house on a date! Away from my overpowering dad and emotionally distant mom. Away from my preoccupied sisters and preferred brothers. I was awe-struck by John, and in no time at all, he told me that he craved time with me and loved having me in his life. I, in turn, fell head over heels for him.

I felt like I'd suddenly been swept into adulthood. With John I wasn't seen as a bothersome sister or a little child or a poor student. I was a woman. And John was no scrawny, immature high school boy. He was a man. John wanted me, and since I craved being wanted, I wanted John. It wasn't long before we became physical. He was clearly experienced, and he knew just what to say and do not only to win my heart and my trust but also to stir my passions.

My father had often said to me that when I started dating, there was no way I was going to get married before all my older siblings were married. Since I still wasn't allowed to date at seventeen, I never took John home to meet my family. That seemed unfair to me because I felt very much like an adult when I was with him.

Adult behavior, however, has adult consequences, as I discovered after months of intense involvement with John. I was pregnant. While it's true I still had very little understanding of how the reproductive system worked, I'd finally learned the big secret about how a girl gets pregnant.

I was frightened when I found out and went to John right away with the news.

His first words? "That baby isn't mine!"

"Of course it is, John. You're the only one I've been with."

Still, he denied the child was his, and suddenly this guy who'd had an insatiable appetite for me couldn't get far enough away. And that was the end of the relationship. He wanted nothing else to do with me. Heartbroken, I left in tears, not knowing where to turn.

After that encounter I learned that John was married with three kids! I'd been duped. Used. I felt stupid and humiliated for believing him.

I didn't know what to do. I didn't know what options I had. So I confided in two very close friends.

"Well, you can't keep the baby. You have to get an abortion," one friend said.

The other nodded knowingly. "Your dad would absolutely kill you if he knew."

Remembering the beating I'd taken for driving away when grounded, I feared he literally would.

I barely knew the facts of life. And I knew nothing at all of pregnancy. So my friends took me to an abortion clinic. Sadly, I was putty in the hands of the people working that day. A doctor and a "counselor" told me that it wasn't even a life yet. "Not enough time has passed for it to become a baby," they each told me. "It's just tissue."

And I bought it because not only did I not know any better, but it was also great news. What a huge relief!

After the abortion, something happened that I wasn't expecting at all. I felt tremendous sadness. A deep sense of loss. I recognized what I was feeling as grief, but why was I grieving if it was nothing but tissue? Why did I feel so empty? Where was my deep sense of loss coming from? I couldn't understand it, but there was no denying it. I felt tremendous guilt—a feeling that wouldn't go away. Beside myself in grief, I decided to go to church and confess to the priest. I needed to talk this out with someone I could trust. Maybe that would make me feel better.

I was still afraid of priests, but I mustered whatever courage I could find and entered the confessional the following Saturday. I wasted no time but got right to the point.

"Father, forgive me for my sins. I got pregnant and had an abortion. Now all I feel is grief and pain and guilt."

There was silence for a few moments; then the priest spoke a few words I don't recall. After that he said, "You'll need to come back in a week for absolution."

I'd hoped he was going to reassure me that it wasn't a baby yet—just tissue. Now I felt frightened. Absolution? Did this mean he had to go to someone else? A more senior priest? If I came back, would someone else be there? Someone who was going to take me away? What did this mean?

I muttered, "Okay," then rushed for the church exit. I couldn't get out of there fast enough.

That was the last time in my life I ever went into a confessional booth. I'd gone with the hope that turning to God would help. Instead, I ran from God's house, believing I'd ruined my relationship with Him.

I was plagued with guilt. I felt dirtier and more wrong and worthless than I ever had. Surely, I believed, I had become everything my family told me I was. Every label they had given me had turned out to be true. I was a failure. A liar. Stupid. Worthless. And now I had a new label I laid on myself—a secret one: I was a woman who had killed her own baby.

The guilt ate away at my soul, and I felt I couldn't live with it. I wanted to die. But I just couldn't act on that feeling. I felt I'd be a failure at being the ultimate failure. So I slugged on, one miserable day after another.

Until one day at school when I saw a poster taped to the wall that said, "Casting for the Spring Play: *Stage Door*."

Even now, looking back, I believe God used that poster to save my life.

●　●　●

I'd never been in a play before. In fact, I'd never had the confidence to get involved in any extracurricular activities. But because of my reputation for being funny, over the next few days several classmates suggested I try out for the humorous character Hattie, the maid in a boarding house for young women trying to break into acting in New York. I decided to go for it, and to my amazement, I won the part!

Being involved in the play was an eye-opening experience for me. I'd never had such a positive time with other schoolmates in my life. I loved learning my part, and I was thrilled to discover that

I was actually good at something. I loved the rehearsals where I felt part of a team—something I'd never experienced. And though I was very nervous when it came time for the real performances, I loved that we were all nervous together. I'd never known such camaraderie before.

Opening night was a great success. The stage props turned out beautifully. The wardrobe was stylish and fun. The script was clever. The audience enjoyed the humor in the dialogue. And I was amazed that it all came together so beautifully. Then, during one performance, I accidently knocked over one of the stage props. I got so frazzled that I forgot my words, but without missing +a beat I improvised a few lines. Hysterical laughter erupted from the audience, letting me know that they loved it. When the play was over, I got a standing ovation! It was my favorite moment of high school. In fact, it became a significant confidence booster that had a major impact on reshaping my social life—an impact I still appreciate to this day.

That performance cemented my reputation for being one of the funniest kids in my class. Not only did many of my class-mates refer to me by that title when they wrote notes in my yearbook, but at the end of the year, they also bestowed on me the coveted "Funniest Girl in the Class" award. It was my first time experiencing a positive image of myself in school. And while this positive experience didn't stop the pain or shame I carried with me every day, it did help me do one thing: hide it. Humor helped me become even more practiced at keeping my secrets and hiding my pain.

* * *

So I'd entered high school as a lonely failure—a reject who'd been kicked out of Catholic school—and emerged from adolescence determined to spread my wings and fly away as fast as I could. Desperate to escape a deeply conflicted home and a sad, fragile heart, I carried a long string of destructive beliefs about myself, all of which I believed I deserved. I'd been deeply wounded from both physical and verbal abuse and had grown accustomed to bearing the brunt of the dysfunction of others.

And so this is the frame of mind I was in when I leaped from my emotionally destitute condition in high school to the job-hunting world, where I was sexually harassed, attacked, and raped. I then drifted from one unhealthy relationship to another until I found myself in a bar, where I met the charming Charlie.

Predators have a keen ability to sense those who are easy prey, and that is certainly what I was. With no one to hope or trust in, and most certainly no confidence in myself other than my acting ability, I placed my hope and trust in Charlie, until I found myself alone and abandoned in a cheap Florida motel. By then, my judgment was so weak and my vulnerabilities so exposed that I'd landed behind bars—first in a police station and finally in a human trafficker's lair.

The simple truth is that I had spread my wings to fly, not knowing that they were already broken.

Part 4

"IN THE LIFE"

1973–1975

9

THE NIGHTMARE

I WAS SITTING ON THE EDGE OF THE BED this particular morning when I heard Danny's footsteps in the hallway approaching my door. Groggy, with a pounding headache from being drugged, I had wrapped myself in a sheet to restore some sense of modesty. I'd already searched the room for my clothes, but all I'd been able to find were the clothes Danny had placed in the closet—like the tight black dress he had tossed in the room the previous night before some stranger expecting sex walked in calling me "Nancy." I couldn't stomach the idea of wearing it or any of the other immodest outfits Danny evidently considered sexy, so the sheet would have to do. Clearly, he had no plans to return my own clothes.

Danny walked in, pocketing the room key. *What next?* I

wondered, bracing myself. *What will it be this time? Another beating? Another rape? Another "client"?*

"I'll bring you some breakfast in a few minutes," he said. "Here's what you'll wear today." He tossed some underwear, a pair of jeans, and a T-shirt on the bed. I didn't move. I just watched him.

"What day is it? And what time?" I asked. I'd lost all sense of the passage of time. Had I been here four days? Five? I wasn't sure. How much longer would this nightmare go on?

"Saturday. It's ten o'clock now. You'll be free until five this evening," he said. "I'll bring you some towels for a shower." It was the most information I'd been given since the day I'd woken up here. That was the day he'd given his speech while I sat on the bed in disbelief and terror.

"You're going to work for me now," he'd said matter-of-factly. "You belong to me. Your name is now Nancy. Nancy Williams. I run an escort service, and you are one of my escorts. I'll be bringing clients to you. Your job is to make them happy."

Panicked, I'd tried to rush for the door, but he'd easily grabbed me, slapped me hard on the side of the head, and thrown me back onto the bed. "You can make this easy, or you can make it hard," he said.

It's sad to write this, but in that instant, I'd thought of my family, and of how, because of them, I knew what it was to be slapped hard by a man. It was familiar. I'd long ago learned the cost of fighting back and the wisdom of cooperating. So I'd decided to submit. I'd bide my time and see if I could escape later. Outright defiance was just going to get me hurt.

Now here I still was—several days held captive in, of all places, an ordinary suburban home, by an ordinary guy-next-door type. I hadn't been allowed to leave this room, and my clothing and identity had been stolen. (I hadn't seen my purse with my driver's license since I'd been released from jail.) I'd been raped, beaten, and drugged more times than I knew. I'd also been compliant at times, because the simple truth was that it hurt a lot less. Unspeakable things had been done to me in those few days. For a split second, I felt a wave of nausea hit me as I started to think along that path, so I shook my head and tried to think of something else. And what I thought of were the drugs.

Danny had forced me to take drugs frequently. I didn't know what kind they were, only that they made me feel high or woozy or sleepy. And I suddenly had a thought that surprised me: *I hope he gives me those drugs again before the next client.* Though I hated the thought of it, I'd discovered how much they helped. Whenever I took those drugs, my mind would float away while my body was being used and abused. They helped me forget about what was being done to me, about what would happen in the days and nights ahead. In a matter of days, I'd become dependent on them. I couldn't face being held captive like this without the drugs to help me through it.

Held captive, I thought. *How is this even possible? Who could even believe a story like this? How will I ever get out of here?*

• • •

As the hours passed that Saturday afternoon, I felt more clearheaded, like I was coming out of a haze. I'd been kept high most of the time, but maybe Danny hadn't drugged me as much the previous night or that morning. I wasn't sure. But between a few naps, I gave a lot of thought to what had happened in the hours before I'd been brought here. I had no answers. Just questions.

Had Hank, my customer at the restaurant, been genuine when he'd offered me the money to go home for the holidays, or was that part of some elaborate trap?

Why did the police come out of nowhere and descend on me in Hank's car, "coincidentally" with the money in my hands?

What had happened to Hank that day? Did he get arrested too? If not, why didn't he come bail me out?

Why had Danny shown up and bailed me out? Who was Danny, really? He said my boss, Glen, had asked him to come get me. Was that true? If so, how had Glen known I'd been arrested? And why would he have sent a stranger to get me—a dangerous stranger who had tricked and abducted me?

Was Glen part of this mess somehow? Or was a dirty cop involved? Had a cop tipped Danny off that there was some defenseless girl in custody who had no one to call? A girl he could pick up cheap, for the two-hundred-dollar bail?

The more questions I thought about, the angrier I got. Because I had no answers. No evidence. No advocate or protector. Other than the fact that I hadn't shown up for work for several days, no one in the world even knew I was missing. My roommate had moved out, and my coworkers probably just assumed I'd found another job and moved on.

I'm the perfect victim, I thought. *No one is even missing me. This is hopeless.*

•   •   •

One day when I woke up, Danny was in my room setting up a video camera in the corner.

"What's that for?" I asked.

"Good business," he said. "Just ignore it." Then he turned and looked at me with a threat in his eyes. "But don't forget about it. If you ever leave this place, just remember I'll always have videos of you as proof that you're just some willing prostitute for hire. Some wannabe porn star."

After that, there were times I was with a client when the camera was on. Was Danny making videos to blackmail a client? Or to make some extra money on the side? Or was it to blackmail me, should I ever escape?

Days turned into weeks. And weeks into months. I honestly can't say how long I was held captive in the innocent-looking suburban house. But I can say that two things happened. One was that I slipped into a horrible depression. Many days I wanted to die. I was trapped in despair. At the same time, I began working to win Danny's trust so I could find a way out of this miserable enslavement. Over time, my plan seemed to work. Danny began rewarding me for good behavior, allowing me out of my room and into the kitchen and living room for brief periods while he was home. I tried to "reward" him in return by tidying up the house and cleaning. This helped me as much as it did him. How awful that it was such a tremendous relief to have something to do other than service strange men—to invest myself in a small, productive activity.

Once I proved myself useful, he increased the length of time outside my room. Then he stopped locking my room. Eventually I was given the run of the locked house when Danny was home. Finally, after what seemed like several months, I was given that freedom when Danny left the house for brief outings. But while he was gone, so was the phone. This was before mobile phones, of course, so he'd unplug the phone from the wall and just take it with him.

During these unchaperoned periods in the house, I searched and snooped, hoping to find anything that might prove useful. Certain kitchen drawers were kept locked. He likely kept knives and sharp objects and household tools in these places. There were also several locked closets.

One day while he was out running errands, I checked the front door as I always did and found it unlocked! My heart started pounding, and I nearly ran out the door on the spot. Then a thought stopped me dead in my tracks: *What if this is a trap? What if he's waiting, in hiding, to see if I try to leave?* It was a terrible dilemma: Should I run and face the risk of getting caught and beaten, or should I stay and prove my trustworthiness so he'd lower his guard even more? I decided to play it safe and stay put—and keep my eyes out for a future opportunity to escape.

He said nothing about the door when he returned an hour or so later. Had I shown myself worthy of greater trust, or had I let an opportunity for freedom slip through my fingers? Later that night, after a client had left, I wept myself to sleep wondering if I'd squandered my only chance to escape.

●　●　●

Months after I was taken captive, my compliance finally paid off. One day I again found the door unlocked. I quickly ran from room to room and checked the view from every window to see if I could spot Danny or his car or any other evidence that he was having the house watched. All clear! I was wearing a pair of short shorts, a clingy T-shirt, and a pair of platform high heels that Danny had given me. Other than the clothes he had placed in my closet, I had nothing.

This was my chance! I stepped outside, closed the door behind me, and took off running.

Within moments I realized how ridiculous it was to run in platform heels, so I kicked them off and kept on running, my bare feet slapping the rough pavement.

I didn't know where to go. I was too fearful to turn to Danny's neighbors, afraid that some of them might be his friends or coconspirators. All I knew for sure was that I wanted to get as far away from Danny's house as possible. He might return at any moment, or even drive right past me. I needed *distance*.

There were no businesses nearby—just houses. The neighborhood had windy roads and cul-de-sacs, and in no time at all, I became disoriented. Though I hadn't run far, the more I ran, the more frightened I became. What if he was already driving around looking for me? What would he do to me if he caught me? Panic was setting in.

Suddenly a taxi drove by. He passed me, then pulled over just in front of me and rolled down his driver's window. I came to an abrupt stop, breathing hard, then slowly approached the car.

"Miss," said a fortyish man, "are you okay? Do you need help?"

That was all the invitation I needed. I all but dove into the back seat of the taxi and slid down low in the seat. I had no idea who this guy was or how I was going to pay for a taxi ride. I barely considered the possibility that this taxi driver was another predator on the lookout for easy prey. I just knew one thing: I had to get away from Danny—quickly—and this man seemed to be the only way out.

"Please," I said in desperation, "get me out of this neighborhood, fast!"

"You've got it," he said. "What direction are you heading?"

"Just away from here," I said, and within moments I was watching the neighborhood I'd been staring at through black bars for months fade from view in the rear window—its image blurred by tears of relief.

10

THE TAXI DRIVER

AS THE TAXI PULLED OUT OF THE NEIGHBORHOOD and into the business district, with me hovering low in the back seat, I broke into sobs of relief. *Is this nightmare really over?* I thought as I watched the rooftops of houses and businesses fly by the windows. With the neighborhood of my imprisonment now out of sight, I dared to sit upright. It seemed too good to be true.

Nothing seemed real. Other cars drove past us with people in them just going about their business. Stores along the road were open, with people going in and out of their doors. How was it possible that life had been going on as usual while I'd been held captive right in the midst of this seemingly normal community? And I'd actually escaped by just walking out the front door and running through the streets? I suddenly felt overwhelmed with gratitude for the taxi driver. If it weren't for his kindness in stopping and offering to help me, my captor might already have picked me up and dragged me back into that house—back into my nightmare.

What now? I suddenly wondered. I had no plan. How could I have spent so many months in that house and not come up with a plan for what I'd do when I broke free? But I'd never believed I would escape. I'd been hopeless.

The driver interrupted my thoughts with a question similar to the one he'd asked when he picked me up: "Miss, where are you going? Are you in some sort of trouble?"

I looked down at my bare feet, short shorts, and tight T-shirt and realized I couldn't just have him drop me off on some street corner.

I gave him the address of my apartment, where I had lived with a roommate before my arrest. The driver offered to wait while I checked it out. I had no idea what to expect there, and my mouth went dry as I approached the door and knocked.

A stranger opened the door—a man. I explained that I used to live there and was hoping to find my belongings. He replied that he and his girlfriend were new tenants and knew nothing about my property, but he kindly called the landlord for me. The landlord told me he had all my belongings but wouldn't release them unless I paid him the thousands of dollars in back rent. This was impossible. I begged for my clothes and personal things, but he wouldn't budge. So I returned to the taxi empty-handed.

In the years since that day, having told many people my story, I've been asked time and again why I didn't just ask to be taken to the police station. A fair question. But given what I'd experienced months before, I couldn't overcome the instinctual sense that the police had somehow conspired to get me into this mess to begin with. How could I, with no identification, no shoes, and no decent clothes, possibly expect the police to take me seriously? I was afraid of them. After all, I'd been conditioned all my life to fear authority figures. No one in authority really had my best interests at heart. And yet this thoughtful stranger driving the taxi had shown me kindness. I'd get his advice on what to do next.

And so I started talking.

I told him about the generous customer who'd offered me a free trip home, the strange arrest, and the bizarre circumstances when Danny had shown up to bail me out and then abducted me and forced me into prostitution. (I still hadn't heard the words *sex trafficking* and had no idea there was even a name for what I'd been through.)

The taxi driver kept shaking his head in disbelief.

"Miss, my name is Jim. Jim Middleton. Where are you from?"

"New Jersey," I said. For a moment, I felt a wave of panic. Danny had drummed into me that I should never tell a client where I was from. Then I assured myself that this man wasn't a client. He was a taxi driver! A kind man.

"Hey, that's where I'm from! Trenton."

I felt a rush of relief, as if I'd just met up with an old neighbor. I felt connected to him right away.

"My name is Gina," I told him, violating another of Danny's rules. It felt good, though, to speak my real name.

"Well, Gina, it sounds like you need a place to stay. And a job, so you can get yourself back home."

"That sounds about right," I agreed. It didn't occur to me at the time that this was an *especially* kind taxi driver. Didn't he know I had no money?

"I could help you get back on your feet," Jim continued. "I have a friend who owns a few furniture businesses. He could probably get you a job in one of his showrooms. I live in the Miami area, which isn't far. Would you like to come to my place so I can contact my friend Sal?"

I couldn't believe this stranger was being so kind. Looking back, I recognize how odd a proposal it was. Still, I had no other options. So, with gratitude, I agreed.

His place was modest, yet comfortable. He led me into the kitchen, gave me a snack, and told me to make myself at home; then he disappeared into another room to call his friend.

"I just talked to my friend Sal," Jim said when he came back. "I've arranged for you to meet him at a hotel bar near here this evening to talk about a job. The bar is close to his showroom and only walking distance from here."

This was more than I could have hoped for—to have a job interview so quickly. But there was no way I could do an interview dressed like this. I explained that to Jim.

"Not a problem," he said. "We've got time to run out and get you an outfit. Lots of shops right here in this part of Miami. I'll pay for it, and you can pay me back from your first paycheck."

We hit a few shops, and in the second one, I was pleased to find a professional-looking skirt, a modest blouse, and a coordinating jacket. We were back at Jim's place in about ninety minutes. In no time, I was showered and dressed for success. Jim clearly enjoyed being a Good Samaritan, and I was nearly euphoric that something was finally going my way. In a matter of only a few hours, thanks to the kindness of a stranger, I felt as if the entire trajectory of my life had shifted. Hope sprang up in my heart, a feeling I hadn't felt in a long time. I was amazed that my crushed and traumatized heart still knew how to hope!

That evening, Sal was professional and very friendly. He liked what I told him about working at my father's jewelry store and about my father's work ethic and customer service. By the end of the interview, Sal offered me a job in his showroom.

"I'm excited you'll be joining the team, Gina! Let's celebrate." He stood and motioned for me to stand too. Expecting to seal the deal with a handshake, I rose. "Come join me in my room for a drink," he said.

"Oh. No, thank you. But thanks so much for the job," I said, extending my hand. He seemed genuinely surprised but took my hand anyway. As he did, I felt a vague discomfort, because rather than a firm business handshake, he gently caressed my hand between both of his. And he invited me again to his room. I declined politely a second time, withdrew my hand, said my good-byes, and headed out the door to walk back to Jim's place. Not sure of my own perceptions and yet feeling uneasy, I walked quickly and didn't look back. Was he simply an affectionate man and a kind boss who wanted me to feel welcome? Or was that invitation to his room loaded with pressure?

I'm probably just imagining sexual innuendo where there isn't any, I thought. *Given all I've been through, that isn't surprising.*

I was eager to thank Jim for helping me get the job, but he wasn't home when I arrived. When he returned a short time later, I could tell that something had drastically changed. It was as if he was a completely different person. Gone was the kind smile. He walked up to me and punched me in the stomach, knocking the wind right out of me. My knees buckled, and I hit the floor. Then came something all too familiar. He beat me. Kicks. Punches. Slaps. Violent shaking. I was in such shock at first that I was like a rag doll in his hands. It reminded me of the beatings I'd gotten as a child. Then I snapped into self-protection mode and tried to get away. I was scrambling toward the door when I felt something sharp against my back. A knife, I assumed, and I was right. I stopped resisting and stood completely still.

Spewing insult after insult, he told me he had expected me to have sex with his friend who had offered me the job. "He paid me for that!" he said.

My world started to spin. I felt nauseous. How could this be happening? So this had been a setup? He'd been plotting this all day? I'd been duped again? How could this possibly be real?

Beaten and bloodied, I was trapped once again in a man's home, fearing for my life.

"But my job with Sal?" I asked, already knowing the answer. It had been a lie from the beginning. How could I have fallen for that? And why had Jim even allowed me to think that was a possibility?

"Forget it, Gina. You're going to be working for me now."

In less than twenty-four hours, I'd gone from the lair of one trafficker to that of another.

• • •

And so began my life with Jim, the taxi driver. He spelled out our vile new arrangement: "You're mine now," he said, "and you work for me. I'll set you up with clients, and you'll do for them whatever they want you to do. Whatever money you earn from those clients is my money, not yours."

He would take me various places in the Miami area and deliver me to men who had paid him for the chance to use me. Jim handled all the money. And he kept me on a very short leash—there was no real chance to escape. Even if I had, how far would I have gotten with no money and no identification? I'd tried that when I'd run from Danny's place.

Eventually I would learn the word for my experience: *trafficking*. But at the time, Jim told me that he and Danny were called pimps, and I was a prostitute. What I needed to learn was how to extricate myself from the arrangement.

How long was I with Jim? I have no idea. I often didn't know what day of the week it was. Every day was as bad as every other day. There were no weekends or holidays or seasons. I had no sense of time. Most of the clients I saw while I was with Jim were interchangeable. I paid as little attention to them as possible. Why would I pay attention to hair color or height?

But then came a day when Jim set me up with a man who was very different from his other clients. For one thing, he arranged to meet me in the lobby of a very nice hotel. "I'd like to take you shopping," he said when we met, and off we went to some very nice boutiques. He bought me a classy white suit with a skirt and jacket. The fabric was silky and elegant. Then he said, "We're going to the racetrack. And I want you to walk with your head held high, as if you have every right to be there."

I'd never felt so beautiful. We didn't go to his room—he never even hinted that we would. Instead, he took me to a clubhouse at the racetrack. There, he ordered us a delicious dinner. He treated me like a lady—as if it were a date. We chatted and laughed. It was such an enormous change for me to be treated with respect. He seemed as if he actually enjoyed my company!

It was my first time at a horse racetrack. I had thought it would be like a dark, dirty bar. It was actually much nicer, although there was a lot of drinking. And it was huge, with vast hallways and grandstands and many places to get food and drinks. I could smell beer and fried food everywhere. In some areas, like the clubhouse we were in, people were drinking champagne and eating expensive food.

After dinner, the man gave me some money to bet on a race. Since I'd never done it before, he told me exactly how to place the bet. I realized, of course, that any winnings would be his, just like the money he'd given me to bet with. We watched several races, and the generous man bought us drinks as we watched. He bet on horses in several races—some won, some lost—but finally, in the last race, the horse he'd told me to bet on was running. We cheered and screamed all through the race, and to my amazement, the horse we'd bet on won! We went up to the window and collected his winnings, which, as it turned out, was a *lot* of money. I expected him to keep it all, but immediately he counted out ten thousand dollars and handed it to me. In cash. *Ten thousand dollars!*

"Take this now and go," he said. "Pack up whatever you have and leave that pimp behind. You deserve a life of your own." Then he did something I found a little strange. He grabbed a napkin and drew a clockface at three o'clock. "Your life is a quarter over. The clock keeps ticking. Make the most of it. You can't take it back."

Who *was* this guy? I had no idea. But I thought of him as an angel. He not only treated me well, but he gave me a lot of money and encouraged me to claim my freedom.

I intended to do just that. I gave my "angel" a heartfelt hug and a peck on the cheek, then turned and scurried away. I ducked into a restroom and hid my cash in the waistband of my skirt so no one would rob me on the way out of the racetrack. Then I hurried toward an exit, looking around nervously for the best place to catch a cab. My heart was pounding out of fear that Jim would be following me, but as I hurried across the lobby, I saw no sign of him. Finally I spotted a major exit, took a left out of it, and ran . . . right into the hands of Jim, who'd been waiting for me.

Jim put an arm around my shoulders as if he were my boyfriend and steered me out into the parking lot. My heart was sinking. I'd thought I was escaping Jim, and now here I was in his clutches again!

As we stood there between the cars, he faced me and said, "Okay, what's going on?"

I didn't want to give up my cash; it was my ticket to freedom, and that kind man had given it to *me*! But I also knew that Jim wasn't going to just let me go. So I told him that his friend had given me some of his winnings, a lot of money, and I had every intention of giving it to him. He held out his hand, waiting. With a lump in my throat, I handed over the ten thousand dollars.

He was overjoyed. I stood there as he focused on counting the stack of bills, wondering what he might do next. When he finished counting, Jim looked up at me and said, "Get back to work."

• • •

I had no idea what to do next. I was too afraid of Jim to just take off. With no place to go in the area, I'd be easy to find and recapture. I ended up getting a ride back to the hotel where I'd met my "date" for the night. I wanted him to know that I'd had to give all the winnings to Jim. While I was sitting in the lobby looking out for him, a woman I'd never met approached me. She was wholesome looking and appeared to be a little older than me.

"May I sit?" she asked. "I'd like to chat with you for a minute." She slid into a chair adjacent to mine. "I can tell you're in trouble," she said quietly. "I think I can help."

I should have been more suspicious, more guarded. But her open, friendly face and apparent wholesomeness appealed to me. I was hungry for a friend—a *woman* friend. I'd already had one "angel" try to help me that day, so why not two? I seldom gave God a thought throughout this dark phase of my life, but I remember thinking about this woman, *Maybe God sent her to me.*

Her name was Candace. Soon we were talking like old friends. She asked lots of questions, and I gave open, unguarded answers. After so many months of spending time only with my pimps or my clients, I found it refreshing to talk with someone who didn't appear to want anything from me. She seemed genuinely caring and concerned about the difficulties of my life.

"Gina," she said, "I think my boyfriend and I can help you.

Let me introduce you to him. He's not far away. First, though, you look tired. Would you like to come back to my place and rest?"

That sounded like heaven to me. We left the hotel, and she took me back to the place she was staying. She called it her place, but it turned out to be one of those extended-stay hotels. I slept soundly all night. In the morning I showered, then Candace gave me pair of jeans and a T-shirt to wear. We were going to meet Candace's boyfriend, Melvin, over breakfast.

We got a booth at a nearby diner, and after a few minutes, Melvin joined us. He shook my hand, but he seemed aloof and withdrawn, as if he had something else on his mind. Tall and stocky and wide through the shoulders, with powerful-looking upper arms, he reminded me of a body builder. His skin was swarthy—kind of an olive tone. He ordered a cup of coffee, but I was hungry and ordered breakfast. In that life, you learn to eat when you have the chance. Candace and I did most of the talking. Like the night before, she asked lots of questions about what I'd been through, repeating for Melvin's benefit some of the things I'd shared in our first conversation. And like before, I found myself really opening up.

When I was finished eating, Melvin paid, and we all left the diner and got into his car. That's when everything changed. Melvin peeled out of the parking lot as if we were being chased, and I said, "What's the hurry? Where are we going?"

"Just shut up," Melvin said gruffly.

"What?" I didn't know what to make of Melvin's sudden hostility, so I said, "Candace, what's going on?"

"What's going on," she said, "is that from this point on, your job is to be quiet and do what you're told. And don't ask questions."

Candace, too, had suddenly become a different person. Where was the wholesome woman who'd shown so much concern about the difficulties of my life? "But wait. I don't want—"

"I told you to shut up," Melvin said. "Open your mouth one more time, and I'll close it for you."

The tone of his voice and the look on his face told me he meant it. Confused and scared, I slid back onto the seat and tried to figure out what to do.

We drove for a long time. I didn't know the roads, and since my grasp of geography was pretty shaky, I wasn't even sure which direction we were going. Once again, I couldn't believe what was happening. Just when I thought I was escaping this life, I seemed to be being yanked very much against my will right back into it. What did they want with me? They knew I had nothing—no money, nothing of value. Except my body, and I had no doubt they intended to use me in ways I would do anything to prevent.

Eventually we pulled off the freeway into a rest stop. I knew I'd never have a better chance to get away. They couldn't lock me in the car. Even if they went to the restroom one at a time, I'd have a chance to get away.

Melvin went first. As soon as he disappeared into the dark doorway of the restroom, I yanked on the door handle, hit the door with my shoulder, and was out on the pavement. Candace managed to grab my hair, but I pulled away. I took off across the grass as fast as I could run, hoping that despite my distrust of the police, I would see a highway patrolman or anybody in uniform. But there weren't that many cars in the lot, and they were all just passenger cars.

Candace was bigger than I was, so I thought I'd be faster, but I hadn't gone thirty feet before she slammed into my back, and down I went onto the hard ground. Seconds later, she was on top of me, punching whatever part of my face she could get to. I covered my face with my hands, and she began pulling my hair. She pulled it so hard that I imagined handfuls of it coming out. Still holding big handfuls of my hair, she yanked me to my feet.

"You're going to regret that," she hissed into my ear. "Now let's go." I tried to pull away as she dragged me all the way back to the car, but it was useless while she had hold of my hair. Melvin was waiting for us. He threw me into the back seat and then punched me hard before slamming the door shut.

I remember seeing people in the parking lot standing next to their cars. Some of them were watching us but not making a move. Others pretended not to see or hear us—but of course they did; they couldn't help it. They were just going about their business, heading for their cars or the restroom. Maybe some of them called 911, but no one rushed over to help me.

Once we were all in the car, Melvin delivered a few more punches, showed me the gun he carried in the glove compartment, and made a few threats that I had no doubt he was perfectly willing to make good on. Then once again we were back on the road.

Melvin, as I strongly suspected and was soon to find out for sure, was another pimp. Candace was his recruiter, but she was also a working girl using the nickname Candy.

Looking back, I recognize two factors at work. First was my learning disability. I was slow at processing information and picking up on the clues and environmental cues that others might quickly detect. Second, traffickers are very skilled predators. They know how to identify and stalk prey. And I was easy prey.

Traffickers often hang out at public locations, looking for young people who appear lost, frightened, undernourished, sleep deprived, and possibly under the influence of drugs—all signs of a runaway who might be susceptible to the deceptive kindness of a predator. Traffickers quickly hook their prey with an offer of a hot meal, a job, or a place to stay. These predators approach with what appears to be kindness so that they can study a victim's weaknesses and discern why they're on their own. Traffickers then begin the grooming process, which may include fraud, deceptive coercion, or physical force. Traffickers deceive and manipulate their prey until they've won them over. So victims with disabilities, like me, make perfect prey. Each of my traffickers quickly had me believing that they really cared about me. Candace had no doubt identified me as an easy mark in the hotel lobby. Hotel lobbies, after all, are fruitful places to look for women like the kind I was then.

We gassed up at the next exit, but with the pain still throbbing from my beating at the rest stop and my bruises already starting to turn purple, I made no attempt to escape. Besides, Melvin stood right beside the car the entire time.

Then we were on the road again, but to where? All I knew at the time was that once again I'd been tricked and abducted against my will, that Candace and Melvin weren't who they pretended to be, and that I had lost what little hope I'd had that I would ever escape again.

11

THE ABYSS

HOW MANY TIMES CAN ONE PERSON fall into the same trap? How could anyone be so gullible? My family was right about me after all. They'd been right all along. And now, riding through the Southeast in the back seat of Melvin's car, a prisoner once again, I not only heard the echoes of their taunts; I joined in with them.

Gina, you are so incredibly stupid. How can you be such an idiot? You have no one to blame but yourself.

The shame of having the same lack of judgment, repeating the same mistakes, and ending up yet again as a patsy, an easy mark, a fool, a sitting duck—a prisoner—was more than I could endure.

I'm disgusted with myself. I deserve my fate. I am a worthless excuse for a human being.

This internal dialogue repeated itself over and over as the miles passed outside my window. I loathed myself, and the more I contemplated how easily I'd been tricked and manipulated, the angrier I became. Not at my various captors. Not at the vile and disgusting men who'd used and abused me. Not even at Candace, my only female trafficker. I was angry at myself. Whatever was yet to be done to me I figured I fully deserved. I was a worthless piece of trash.

I'd love to say that driving headlong into even more abuse, I suddenly had an epiphany, recognizing how I'd been groomed since childhood to be a victim; how my learning disabilities had left me unable to discern subtle deceptions, obscure clues, and hidden motives; how I'd never been taught how to set safe boundaries and enforce them, or even that I deserved to have them; how I'd seen myself as a punching bag, the butt of jokes and insults, a toy for others' sexual misbehavior. But I can't write that. I had no such epiphany. I absolutely believed all these messages from the first twenty or so years of my life. The problem *was* me. The fault *was* mine. I was now certain of it. And what little fight I'd had in me had just been used up when I was overpowered and dragged by my hair back into this cage on wheels.

Now, years later, I'm often asked, "Why did you stay? Surely you could have run. You could have escaped. Couldn't you have fought more? Couldn't you just refuse to be used that way?"

I do sometimes wrestle with those questions. But at the time, it was impossible to imagine. I had no options. No way out. Run where? In what direction? Escape to what? Refuse at what cost? I owned absolutely nothing. I didn't even own the slutty clothes and ridiculous shoes I was usually forced to wear. Just the thought of being beaten to a pulp was usually enough to keep me in line.

Besides, there were the drugs. In the trafficking world, captors and clients alike use drugs to manipulate you. They use drugs to lure you. They use drugs to threaten you. Even though at first you don't want them, eventually you become addicted. Drugs foster compliance, so you don't even dream of fighting back. You come to welcome the drugs because, under their influence, you don't feel anything. Your mind becomes disconnected from your body, and you become a mannequin. You live in nothingness, connected to nothing. Yes, there were times I did resist or run—only to get the defiance beaten out of me. Such pain seemed useless.

I think of the next period of my life as *the abyss*. I lost all sense of time and place. Melvin and Candace had no true home base (that I knew of), except their car. We traveled from town to town, state to state, stopping anywhere from ritzy hotels to cheap fly-by-night motels. Candace was my watchdog. She always knew what room I was in and where they'd be taking me next. Only when I wasn't in some hotel or motel room with a nameless, faceless man did we take time to relax, eat, freshen up, and sleep. I was their meal ticket, their entry pass, and they collected and handled all the money (rarely did I even see the exchange), just as they masterminded the contacts and the calendar. Apart from the rising and setting of the sun, I often didn't know the time of day or night, much less the day of the week or even the month. It was all a blur. A miserable, exhausting, wretched blur of one dehumanizing, disgusting act after another. Food, sleep, drugs, abuse, and threats were all used as rewards or punishments.

Through it all, my captors made it crystal clear that I was to please the client at all costs. It was usually Candace, though sometimes Melvin, who talked with the client while collecting my fee. Afterward, I might be rewarded with a meal, extra sleep, or extra drugs if the client was very pleased. If he wasn't, I was slapped around or told I'd be going hungry or would get no drugs because of my underwhelming performance. As disgusting as it sounds to describe myself in this way, I was like a trained dog. I learned to perform well. I hate even typing these words, but it's the simple, undeniable truth.

That was the abyss. A shapeless, timeless, bleak existence in which I floated day after week after month.

•   •   •

One day, most likely after about a year of living in the abyss with Melvin and Candace, we pulled into the Atlanta area. Candace explained that there was a conference in town that usually produced a steady stream of clients. Melvin dropped Candace off at a little clothing shop, then returned in about thirty minutes to pick her up. She'd bought fresh outfits for us. Then we stopped at a nice hotel and checked in. After Candace and I showered and made ourselves up, Melvin drove us to another upscale hotel and dropped us off at the conference center, where we were to "work" together looking for clients. We'd been there about an hour or so when suddenly a man I was chatting with pulled out a badge with one hand and handcuffs with the other. Before I knew it, my wrists were cuffed behind my back, and an undercover cop was arresting me. This time I understood what *prostitution* and *solicitation* meant. (Sadly, I'd learned quite a few other things during that period of my life.) I was taken outside and loaded into the back seat of a police car. I tried to spot Candace, to send her some signal, but with no luck.

Suddenly it occurred to me, *This is my chance to get help and find safety. I'll tell the police the truth and give them my real name.* I actually felt the nearly forgotten sense of hope rising in my chest as I was driven to the station.

I was probably high or drunk at the time, because my memories of my arrest are foggy and vague. I don't remember much about the drive or arriving at the station, but eventually I found myself alone in a cell. At first, I was relieved that no one else was in there with me—it was peaceful and quiet. That changed quickly, because while I was alone, where no one else could see, a uniformed officer entered, raped me, and left. I was livid. Yes, I'd been forced to have sex many times before, and had, in fact, been brutally raped more than once, but this was different. This was the *police department.*

I'd allowed myself to truly *hope* I'd meet some honest cops who could help me. Now those hopes were dashed, and I was furious to find myself victimized once again by someone who was supposed to be a good guy.

I started to yell. Loudly. I screamed until an officer I hadn't seen before came rushing to my cell.

"What is it?" he asked. "What's the matter?"

"One of your officers just raped me!" I shouted. "Right here! Just minutes ago!" The cop looked a bit rattled. "I want to speak to your boss!" I insisted.

For a moment he stood there and said nothing. I imagined he was thinking through his options.

"Ma'am," he finally said, "you could tell my boss, but no one's going to believe you."

When he said that, an old memory came to mind. The memory of when I'd been playing in my room as a young child, and a male from the pack (someone who should have been trustworthy) had jumped me, pinned me to the bed, and molested me. He'd warned me to tell no one, that no one would believe me, but I ran off to my mother immediately, as he calmly followed. And he'd been right. My mother hadn't believed me, and he'd gotten off with no consequences. I'd felt voiceless and betrayed.

Now, as I stood face to face with an uncertain-looking young officer with metal bars between us, I threw my shoulders back and stepped forward. My usual habits until that point in my life had been to back down, avoid conflict, and play my part as the helpless victim. Was it the drugs or alcohol in my system? Or the memory of the injustice from my childhood? Or the hope stirring in me that being here, in this place at this time, might win me my freedom? To this day, I have no idea. But I stepped forward again, my nose nearly at the bars and shouted, boldly, "I want to see your boss."

"Okay, calm down. I'll be back," he said. A few minutes later he returned and said, "Follow me."

At this point my emotions were wildly churning. I couldn't help but think he was taking me someplace where *he* could attack me. Still, I felt hopeful that I'd be taken to someone who had the authority to help me with my larger problem—being trafficked.

"Where are you taking me?" I asked.

"To see my boss."

Out of my cell, down a hall, and a few turns later, I was ushered into the office of a man in authority. I'll refer to him as "the commander." "What's the matter?" he asked.

"One of your officers raped me in my cell." I stated it as simply and directly as I could.

The commander stared directly into my eyes for a moment. I then gave him my name and said I was being forced to be a prostitute. He sat on the edge of his desk, and when he finally spoke again, he was calm and clear.

"Well, we're going to let you go. Now. But you're never going to come back to this state again."

And that is exactly what happened. I was immediately escorted out of his office, taken to a desk where an officer sorted and stamped some papers, and then taken out an exit where, to my horror, Melvin and Candace sat in their car waiting for me. Candace jumped out, took my arm, and escorted me to the back seat. I was so stunned at seeing her waiting for me there that I was speechless. Melvin drove us away, and the next thing I knew, we were on an interstate heading out of Georgia.

It soon became clear that the incident had left the two of them furious with me. Had I known when I'd climbed into their car outside the police station what was awaiting me in the next town, I would have fought for my life to get away from them.

I don't know what state or town we were in when we stopped, although it was obvious my traffickers knew exactly where we were headed. Neither of them spoke to me during the drive. When we arrived at a motel, Melvin took care of the registration. When he came back to the car with the keys, he told Candace their room number.

"You go on to our room, Candy," he added, handing her one of the keys. "I'm taking Gina to hers." Then, holding up the other key, he barked at me, "Room 212. Lead the way."

When we arrived at my room, he unlocked the door and shoved me in, locking the door behind me. I knew in my gut what was about to happen. I ran to the toilet and was vomiting when the room door suddenly flew open. Melvin sent a man in, and the door slammed behind him.

Nothing good would come of describing what the next several hours were like, other than to say that my traffickers had decided to teach me a lesson by gathering up several men to rape and beat me. I thought I would surely die during the ordeal. I certainly wanted to.

I still live with unanswered questions about the events in Georgia and what happened afterward. How did Melvin and Candace find me? How long had they been sitting in the parking lot at the police station? What happened, if anything, to the officer who had raped me? I still wonder if the commander believed me. I like to think that if he'd heard my story in full that day—the story of my being trapped and trafficked, he might have helped me.

But that morning, as Melvin and Candace drove me away from Georgia, all I could do was stifle the tears. Hope was snuffed out once more.

I believe my heart grew harder that day. I learned that hope, when it rises, exposes the heart to the risk of being crushed all over again. And a crushed heart hardens. I don't recall hoping much after my time in Georgia and the horrific night that followed. I was through with it.

I was done with hope.

12

LIFTOFF

"NEXT STOP: LAS VEGAS," Melvin announced one morning as the three of us took our usual places in the car.

"I love Vegas," Candace said to no one in particular. "Haven't been back for a long time. A few years. That was before you were working with us. Ever been there, Gina?"

I bit my tongue before saying anything snide about my "working with" them, as if I did so willingly. And "a few years" irritated me too. It had probably been around a year and a half since they'd abducted me. But the last thing we needed right now was an argument or tempers flaring.

"No. What do you love about it?" I honestly wasn't the least bit interested in why Candy liked Vegas. I despised her and the empty life she lived. As for my own life, I'd come to accept that I was nothing—just a commodity to be sold and used again and again.

I was just trying to appease them by letting them hear whatever they wanted to hear to avoid being smacked around.

We'd been going through a tough spell. Our last few stops hadn't been as lucrative as most, and the two of them blamed that on me. Who knows? Maybe they were right. I certainly knew the difference between merely fulfilling a client's request and leaving him wowed. I hadn't been doing much wowing lately, and I knew it. I also knew that if I wasn't enticing new clients to want my services, I was likely to get beaten again, have drugs withheld, or left hungry for a day or two.

The first step in the punishing process was a tongue-lashing, which Melvin and Candace had given me the night before. Melvin had been threatening for a few months to get me pregnant so he could sell the baby. My fear of him was growing. I was hitting bottom and knew it. I saw no way out of this life but death—either from Melvin or from a client beating or from suicide, which I was thinking more about these days. I was also strung out, exhausted, and tired of feeling dirty inside and out.

"I love the lights and the energy," Candace said. "And the shows! Gina, if this is a good stop for you, we've decided we'll take you to a nice show on your last night here. How does that sound?"

"Thanks. I appreciate that. I'm sure it's going to be a good stop for us." I hoped I sounded believable. I sure didn't feel it.

I could see that Candace was trying to lighten the mood after our confrontation the night before. And I was trying to do the same. I decided to tell them what I knew they wanted to hear.

"I hadn't realized I'd been slipping. But now that you've pointed it out to me, I can snap out of this low."

"Good thing, Gina," Melvin said. "We need a few banner nights, and Vegas is the best place for it. People come here to feel good, and they're ready to pay for it. But there's lots of competition, so you've got to really shine. I'll be close by to handle business."

Those last words were said in a threatening tone of voice and brought a nightmarish memory to the front of my mind of the punishment I'd received when I'd been arrested for prostitution in the Atlanta area, and Melvin and Candace were waiting at the police station just as I was released. I knew it was no coincidence that on the heels of a sound scolding the night before Melvin was threatening me with that old memory on our way to Vegas. I wanted to convince him I'd remember that he was boss.

•   •   •

Hours later, after driving across desert roads, we checked into a swanky Vegas hotel, and I had time to shower, manicure my nails, and rest for about half an hour. Then I left to work at another hotel. *They're going to be happy with me.* I'd make sure of it. I casually stopped by the craps table to watch the game. I took my time making eye contact with various men and showing interest in the game and the players.

One man playing craps randomly started talking to me and said, "Hey, where are you from?"

For some reason I'll never understand, I once again said what I wasn't supposed to say: "New Jersey."

"Oh? The friend I'm with is from New Jersey too. Whereabouts in Jersey?"

Again, without a thought, I heard myself say "North Jersey." *What is wrong with me?* I knew the rules about never giving out real identifying information.

He did a double take. "She's from there too," he said. "What are the chances?" He was a bit drunk and sounded overly excited about the coincidence.

Yeah, right, I thought. *Sure she is.* My paranoia suddenly kicked in. *Is Melvin setting me up? Gathering evidence against me so he can come down hard on me tonight?*

Then the man said, "Terri is up in my room. I'll introduce you to her. Let's go up."

"Oh, no thanks," I said. I wasn't going to fall for that trick again. "I'll just stay put and watch the game."

"Fine. I'll bring her down," he said. "Yeah, she was born and raised in North Jersey. You both have that same Jersey accent."

Terri? I thought, a little surprised. I'd gone to school with a girl named Terri. I'd actually been good friends with her. But I wasn't going to say anything else. There must have been thousands of girls named Terri in North Jersey.

The next thing I knew, the man left the room. Minutes later he returned to the entrance, a woman by his side. But I couldn't get a good view of her through the incoming crowd.

When the crowd between us cleared, my knees nearly buckled. *It is the same Terri!*

She was scanning the room while listening to the man as he whispered something in her ear.

"Terri?" I blurted out. Our eyes met, and hers widened in shocked recognition.

"Gina?" she nearly shouted. And then her face fell as she looked at me, painfully, from head to toe. "What on earth has happened to you? What are you doing here?"

●　●　●

"Well, what are *you* doing here?" I said. "I can't believe it's you!" We were hugging in an instant and talking a mile a minute. At first I tried to deflect her questions and turn them back to her, but then she put her hands on my shoulders, held me at arm's length, and looked me directly in the eyes.

"Gina, what has happened to you?" Our eyes were locked. "Are you okay?" Then she just stood there, waiting for an answer.

One tear slipped from my eye, and I wiped it away as quickly as I could.

"We can't talk here," I whispered. "It's not safe."

"The ladies' room," we both said at once.

I quickly scanned the gaming room to make sure I didn't see Melvin or Candace. All clear for the moment. Meanwhile, Terri whispered in her companion's ear, and he made his way back to the craps table. Then, separately, she and I walked to the ladies' room. I gave a final glance around the gaming room before the door shut behind me.

Like so many of the ladies' rooms in the big Vegas hotels, this one was vast and luxurious. As the door closed behind me, it muffled all the noise in the hallway. A wall of mirrors on one side stood adjacent to a wall of countertops with mirrors and lights. We could both see our reflections in the mirrors as the two of us stood side by side. Terri and I had graduated together, so we were about the same age—twenty-two or twenty-three—but at the time I wasn't even sure how old I was. I'd spent too much time in the abyss. But one thing was sure: I no longer looked as young and fresh as Terri. My two to three years "in the life" had visibly aged me.

I fell into Terri's arms and quietly sobbed. She simply held me and waited. A woman entered the room, and out of shame I stopped sobbing and grabbed some tissues from the box on the counter to wipe my eyes and nose. Suddenly, remembering that Melvin or Candace might already be looking for me, I started to explain my situation to Terri. It's impossible to remember what I said. Like a dam breaking, my words poured out so fast I could barely breathe.

In just a few minutes, Terri had heard enough.

"Gina, I'm going to call your parents. I'll tell them I've found you and that you're desperate to come home. Then we've got to get you out of here and to the airport, immediately."

I looked at Terri in disbelief. I'd lived so long without hope of breaking free, believing there was no way out of this life but death. I had no words. Terri's idea sounded absurd. Crazy. Absolutely impossible.

"Gina, you wait in here. In a stall. Don't come out until I come back for you."

"But where are you going?"

"To the pay phones in the hallway, to call your parents. Now."

"But Terri, this can't work."

She just pointed me to a stall, gave me a little push in that direction, then left.

Locked in the stall, I was afraid that my pounding heart was so loud everyone in the restroom could hear it.

The minutes dragged on and on for so long that I began to worry that Melvin and Candace would find me before Terri came back. But then I heard the door open, and Terri's voice called out softly, "Gina?"

When I opened the stall door, Terri grabbed my hand and then mouthed, "Airport. Now."

I found it hard to breathe as we stepped out of the restroom, doing our best to seem casual and relaxed. Rather than exit through the huge front doors, we took a hallway to a side exit, and when we stepped outside the hotel, there was Terri's guy holding open the door of her car. I climbed in, and Terri took the driver's seat.

"Your ticket is paid for," she said. "Your cousin, a travel agent, got the ticket. Your dad called her and asked if he could get you home from Vegas. All you need to do is go to the ticket counter, pick up your ticket, go to your gate, and wait there. Then get on the plane when they announce it. It's a red-eye, so it will be early morning when you get home."

A few hours later, I was boarding a plane heading east. As the plane lifted off, I stared out the small window. The solid black of the night sky ahead stood in stunning contrast to the lights of Vegas disappearing below me. I couldn't even see any stars. Just deep blackness—like the abyss I'd been living in since 1972.

I must have been in shock. I felt nothing. Not relief from being rescued out of the clutches of Melvin and Candace. Not fear about what I would face the next morning when I'd see my family for the first time in years. Nothing seemed real. I simply felt numb. As if I'd just awakened to learn what year it was.

I'd left home as a wide-eyed teenager, believing I was finally free to spread my wings and fly. But I'd met with disaster at every turn. I'd crashed and burned. What now? What came next? I had no idea. No dreams. No aspirations. No hopes. My heart, my soul, felt as black as the dark night outside my plane window.

Finally, after dozing and waking a few times, I awoke to a surprising sight outside my window: light! In the distance I could see the pale light of dawn pushing back the darkness. And then I wondered if, somehow, on the other side of this flight, there was a future waiting for me. I couldn't imagine what that future might hold. By that time in my life, I was so filled with worthlessness, fear, and shame that I couldn't imagine anything good waiting for me.

But I didn't know then what I know now. I didn't know who held my future in the palm of His hand. And I didn't know I had an enemy who was still determined to keep me captive.

Part 5

INVISIBLE CHAINS

1975–2016

13

SECRETS

There are two kinds of secrets.
The ones we keep from others and the ones we keep from ourselves.
FRANK WARREN

HAD ANYONE NOTICED ME stepping off that plane in Newark, they'd have seen a hollow-eyed twenty-three-year-old in a short, tight skirt, low-cut blouse, and platform shoes, apparently traveling light. No luggage. No carry-on. Not even a purse.

But I certainly didn't feel like I was traveling light. I was bound head to toe in thick, heavy chains, and dragging more behind me. Invisible chains, yes. But real nonetheless.

As my story has shown, every link of those chains had a story to tell. Some of those links had been hung on me in childhood with name-calling and insults, assault and abuse, creating chains of worthlessness and fear and shame. More links had been added with molestation, humiliation, mockery, and failure, interlinked with anger, resentment, bitterness, self-pity, and swallowed rage.

Some were wrapped around my neck, leaving me strangled and voiceless. Clueless, I'd dragged those chains with me to Florida, where the links of self-blame and self-recrimination multiplied with every victimization I experienced. I was to blame. I had it coming. I was the stupid one. I was trouble. I deserved this. The problem was me. The fault was mine.

I arrived "home" feeling no sense of homecoming at all. After all, I'd been fleeing home when I'd moved in with Charlie. That now seemed a lifetime ago. For what it's worth, my perception—which may not have been worth much given my condition—was that my homecoming was seen more as a disruption to the family than a relief. No one knew my story, and to my surprise, *absolutely no one asked!* Not one single person.

As far as my family was concerned, I'd run off to Florida, landed in trouble, become a prostitute, and finally come home a broken failure who had shamed my family's reputation. And because I was so filled with self-disgust, I was too voiceless to tell my story. I wouldn't have known where to even begin. And who would have believed it anyway? Even if they'd decided I was telling the truth, having others know what had taken place would just have multiplied my shame. They never would have been able to look at me again without thinking about how stupid and gullible I'd been to get abducted—multiple times—and how disgusting it was that I'd allowed my body to be repeatedly used and abused.

Even so, on one occasion, I decided to take the risk of telling a member of my family. "I'd really like to share with you what happened to me during that time I was away," I said. My heart was pounding so hard that I was afraid I was going to pass out.

"I don't want to talk about it," she said. "You were a prostitute. A prostitute is a prostitute is a prostitute."

I didn't know what to say. After that, she gave me the silent treatment—a common form of abuse used by my various family members. A short time later, she left town, and that's how our friendship ended. I never saw her again.

A prostitute is a prostitute is a prostitute.

I decided at that point that my friends and family simply had no way to cope with the otherworldly nightmare I'd endured. And I had no interest in revisiting the cesspool I'd swum in during my nightmare years. Who would believe me? How could I describe it to anyone?

So, once again, I chose silence. Let them all think what they wanted. Surely it was better this way. I'd keep my filthy secrets to myself.

Not only did I not know of nor understand the invisible bonds I wore, I had no concept that such chains are magnetic. That we are drawn to the familiar, no matter how broken it is. So, in retrospect, what came next was shockingly predictable.

I needed a job and happened to have an uncle in the nursing-home business who encouraged me to go to a school that offered training in food-service management. So I registered for some courses there. Soon after classes began, I met a man named Larry. I was starved for connection, attention, and escape, and in a whirlwind of a few short months, I discovered I was pregnant. Fear shot through me.

We'd talked about getting married, so I decided to tell Larry about my pregnancy. We were sitting in his car when I told him. He became angry, telling me that if I didn't end the pregnancy, we were done. Clinging to him, I tried convincing him that everything would work out, but he was furious and didn't want to hear it. He pushed me away and started punching me. Then he reached over me, opened my door, and kicked me out of the car and onto the sidewalk.

I miscarried as a result of Larry's beating but comforted myself with the old lies I'd been told at my earlier abortion—that it was just tissue, not a life growing within me.

Not ever wanting to see Larry again, I never went back to my classes. I don't recall being heartbroken; I just felt numb.

Empty.

Welcome to freedom, Gina. More links in my chains. I barely noticed the added weight on my soul.

I was soon job hunting again, and I landed a decent job doing office work in the county social-services department. I thought I'd arrived! Just getting up, showering, and dressing professionally for the day made me feel more worthwhile. I worked hard, made polite small talk with my coworkers, and kept a low profile. Socializing, however, was surprisingly exhausting for me. I simply felt I had nothing in common with my coworkers. They'd chat about family get-togethers and outings with siblings and college or childhood memories. Their weekends sounded full and satisfying. I'd laugh along and pretend it was the same for me, but their lives were foreign to me. And I dared not share the violence of my past or the emptiness of my present. I felt like a fake. Another link added to my chains.

Weeks turned into months, and in spite of feeling like a misfit pretending to fit in, I also felt like this was the most restful and stable few months of my young-adult life so far. If I'd known then what I know now, I'd have recognized that I was far from healthy and balanced. I would have seen the danger signs: Compulsively showering a few times a day to feel clean and yet always feeling dirty. Looking forward to a drink at the end of the day and pills in the evening to quiet my racing thoughts and help me sleep at night. Awakening each morning trying to shake free of the ugly nightmares from my past. Aching with loneliness, especially over the weekends. Unable to break free from the negative self-talk that dominated my thinking.

And that's when I met Ray at work. It started with an occasional drink or dinner after work, and like my relationship with Larry, it moved pretty quickly. Within a few months, we were engaged.

More evidence of how desperately I wanted to *belong*.

• • •

To my surprise, Mom threw herself into wedding planning, and Dad was clearly pleased. This would be no small, quiet wedding. No. This would be a huge celebration. I'm not sure why. Maybe because they felt it was a turning point for me and a chance to go public with the news that I was doing okay. That I was putting my troubled adolescence behind me and had now turned respectable. Maybe it was because Ray's family was successful and socially respected. They were a family of means, and their social standing was important to them. I believe my parents—the town jeweler and his wife—were genuinely happy I'd made it into the good graces of such a family. It probably gave them hope for me, though they never told me so.

Obviously, the story of what transpired during my years away from home was still a secret. Family friends, aunts, uncles, cousins, and the pack had known I'd gone away after high school and then come back, but that was about it as far as I knew.

Invitations went out to my family, many of my parents' friends (a large number of whom I didn't even know personally), and Ray's family, and soon we had RSVPs from more than two hundred and fifty guests. Naturally, it would be a Catholic wedding, with my family's priest officiating, and we'd enjoy an amazing feast by Michele's Catering afterward. My mother and I picked out a gorgeous white wedding gown, and I was genuinely surprised and happy at the fuss being made over me of all people. I'd never before been the object of such a celebration.

During our engagement, I began telling Ray some of my story. One time, after I'd barely said a few words, he replied, "I know about this."

"What? How?"

He mentioned the name of a family member, then said, "She told me what little she knew."

I could think of only one way that person could have known any of the story. Someone else in my family must have shared their idea of why I'd needed my family's help flying home. Prostitution. I was shaken and wondered who else might think they actually knew my story.

Still, I continued telling Ray what had actually happened to me. He must not have heard much from that member of the pack, because the brief version of my real story mortified and stunned him beyond words. Perhaps the most important thing he did was simply *believe* me—a huge relief, since I knew my saga sounded so bizarre. We ended that confidential conversation with his agreement—his promise to me—that he would never, under any circumstances, tell my secrets to anyone else. I trusted his solemn promise.

As the wedding approached, I worked at my relationships with my siblings. I so longed to *belong* in my family, to feel connected and accepted and loved. But since my return home, we'd had an awkward coexistence. I could fill a few pages describing the provocation, insults, and controlling behaviors directed at me. I imagine that, if given the opportunity, they would have said I was trouble. The black sheep. The disrupter. In other words, not much had changed since I'd moved out of the house. It was, I decided, simply our pattern, the way things would always be. As I mentioned before, in our family, the boys were favored over the girls, and the girls were expected to accommodate whatever was thrown our way. None of us knew how to break that pattern. Maybe nobody wanted to break it. So I just tried to accept it as our normal, no matter how uncomfortable it was, and did my best to believe that underneath it all, we loved each other.

An incident on my wedding day paints a picture of how this

complex dynamic between my family members and me worked, and how it made me feel.

It was a beautiful October morning in 1978. I was twenty-six years old and eager to enjoy every detail of my special day. My six bridesmaids had come over to my parents' house to dress and primp before the photographer arrived, so it was quite a mad-house. Our home had only one and a half bathrooms, and it was my turn to take a shower and put on my dress. Just as I was about to step into the full bathroom upstairs, one of my family members squeezed through the crowded hallway, rushed into the bathroom, and shut and locked the door behind him.

I knocked on the door. "It's my turn in there," I called through the door. "The photographer is coming soon, and I have to shower and get dressed in a hurry." I was worried. This person had a repu-tation for taking very long showers and dominating the bathroom for inordinately long periods of time. No answer. Now I pounded on the door.

"This is no joke. We've got everything timed. I need to get in there, now!" Still no response, but I heard the shower turn on.

"Ma," I yelled down the stairs, "I need to be ready for the photographer."

"Oh my," Mom muttered as she came to the foot of the stairs. She called up the stairs rather weakly. "Come on now. It's Gina's turn. She doesn't have time to wait for you. You can use it when she's done."

Nothing.

She wrung her hands and then walked away as if powerless. And maybe she was. I'd hoped she'd march up the stairs, bang on the door, and insist he come out.

I was near tears. *Why today? Of all days, why would he do this to me on my wedding day?* Given all the violations I had suffered, maybe it shouldn't have seemed like such a severe offense. But somehow that incident captured the painful space I held in the family. It felt like a gut punch. Like a slap in the face. *Move over,* this act said to me. *You're nothing. Your special day is nothing to me. Everyone else in this family comes before you, because you are nothing.*

Clearly, the feelings and self-talk were about much more than the timing of a shower or a family member's selfishness. They came from a wounded place deep in my soul—the dark cavern where the wounded child within me huddled, feeling slighted and meaningless and *less than* everyone else. That inner child was always so close to the surface. She was a victim—and nothing more.

Knowing I was powerless to change my circumstances, I grabbed a bag; tossed in my makeup and hair products; gathered my dress, my slip, my hose, and my shoes; and took off for my sister's house a short distance away, tears streaming down my face. I left behind the gaiety and camaraderie and fun of my bridesmaids and got ready all alone at my sister's place. I had no choice.

●　　●　　●

A year passed. I woke to the sounds of a hospital. Machines beeping from some other room drifted in from the hallway. A muffled announcement calling some doctor over the PA system. Hurried footsteps passing my door. Distant conversations. I opened my eyes and tried to turn my head to see if my door was open or shut, but a pain shot through my neck and left shoulder. *My painkillers must have worn off,* I thought. *I hope it's time for my next dose.*

I heard a slight knock on my room's door and turned my head in spite of the pain. The door was barely ajar.

"Yes," I called.

In walked the minister who'd officiated my wedding ceremony. He had a gentle look on his face. "Gina," he said. "I've been worried about you. How are you?" I fought back tears at his compassion for me.

"I'm doing okay, Father," I lied, trying to sound cheerful. "I'll probably get out by tomorrow."

He looked me over with an expression of pity and skepticism. "Really? You look awfully banged up, Gina."

I didn't know how to respond to that. I'd seen my face in the mirror the night before. Bruises. A black-and-purple eye. A cut and swollen lip. And that was counting only the marks on my face. My stomach, my side, and my back also bore wounds from the beating that had landed me here. I was a mess and I knew it.

"Listen," he said. "Ray will keep this up until he kills you. You don't deserve to be treated this way. You need to leave him."

I stared at him, shocked. "Leave him? But I . . . I can't. I don't believe in divorce." I was confused. Did I really have to explain such a thing to a priest? "I need to keep my vows. Besides, I do love him."

"But Gina, this isn't the first time his beatings put you in here. You know it won't be the last."

He was right. Ray's abuse had left me hospitalized twice in our first year of marriage, and that didn't include the bruises I'd nursed and hidden without seeking care. I thought back to my first argument with Ray several months after we'd married. I came home at lunchtime one day. This was unusual for me, and the moment I opened the front door, the smell of marijuana and alcohol smacked me in the face. I was surprised to find that Ray was also home. He jumped up from the couch, and we both started yelling at each other. The truth, he finally confessed, was that he'd been fired for using drugs on the job. I was shocked—as much by his behavior as by the fact that I'd missed the signs of his addictions. Hearing his confession, I felt like I'd won the fight . . . until he struck me in the face with his hand. Ray was a powerful man, and I went flying. I was like a rag doll as he hit me again and again.

I grimaced now at the memory, but I didn't want to discuss any of this with my priest. It was humiliating. I was relieved when he suggested praying for me and then left. I suspected he knew a lost cause when he saw one, and I believed that's exactly what I was. It never occurred to me that his prayer might actually have any power or influence on my life. Not because I didn't believe in prayer. I believed in prayer the same way I believed in God. It was real, just like God was, but it didn't touch my life. It was "out there" somewhere. It was for good people, not trash like me.

•   •   •

A few weeks passed, and Thanksgiving of 1979 was only days away. Ray and I planned to have our Thanksgiving meal with his parents a few days early.

But we were arguing, again. Why was it never long between our explosions of bitter anger? At least this time it wasn't getting physical. I looked at the anger in Ray's eyes and decided I'd better quickly do my best to bring down the tension a notch or two. I did not want another beating. I took a deep breath and softened my voice, and soon we'd lowered the temperature. Finally our argument petered out, though anger still surged through me. I was good at pretending all was fine when, in truth, my anger simmered.

"Look at the time," Ray said. "We need to leave for Thanksgiving dinner at Mom and Dad's in about an hour."

I bristled. There was no way I was going to pull myself together, reapply my makeup—now tear-streaked—and then spend the afternoon with his parents while I pretended everything was fine. I didn't have the emotional energy.

"No, Ray. You go without me. I can't."

The embers of our argument hadn't yet cooled enough, and sparks flew once again, but I held my ground. An hour later he left, alone, slamming the door behind him. I was relieved that he was gone.

Several hours later, I heard his car pull into the driveway. What kind of mood would he be in? I hoped his time with his family had softened him. But nothing could have prepared me for the look on his face when he walked in. Red-rimmed eyes, blotchy skin. Clearly he'd been crying in the car.

"Ray? What's going on?"

"Gina, I'm so sorry," he said.

I thought at first he was apologizing for our earlier argument, but as he talked, all thoughts of that argument faded. He confessed that in his anger at me for not going with him to his parents', he'd complained to them about me. And then he'd done the unthinkable: He'd told them my secret. What I'd confided in him before our marriage and what he'd vowed to never divulge: my nearly three-year nightmare of trafficking, abuse, and forced prostitution long before I met him.

Ray's family was financially well off, and their image meant the world to them. Horror-struck to hear of my soiled past, they'd given Ray an ultimatum on the spot.

"Gina," he choked out as he wept, "they told me that either I divorce you or they will disown me."

Struggling to take in what he was telling me, the only response I could muster was "What are you saying?"

But over the next few minutes, everything became crystal clear. Ray was going to divorce me. The hidden ugliness of my past had been exposed and was going to cost me my marriage.

And so it did.

14

THE CHASE

ANOTHER SIREN? More flashing lights? They seem to be multiply-
ing. They must be chasing somebody. I was flying along the interstate
as one police car after another came up alongside me. I'd already
moved to the right lane so they would pass, but it didn't seem to
help. All the lights flashing in the dark were distracting, and their
sirens seemed unusually loud. Finally I saw an exit ramp coming
up, but it was on the left. *I'll just exit there. Get out of the way of*
this mess, I thought as I cut the wheel to the left.

    What? They're getting off here too? I swore, aggravated.
Unbelievable! I pounded the steering wheel in frustration.

    Suddenly, several patrol cars pulled directly in front of me and
slowed, then came to an abrupt stop. I slammed on the brakes and
screeched to a halt, nearly crashing into one of them.

In a heartbeat, cops were leaping from their cars and approaching my car. Finally it dawned on me in my drunken and drugged stupor that I was the one they'd been chasing! Shaken, confused, and angry, I threw open my door and tried to jump out to face one of the yelling officers, but I stumbled forward, landing in his arms. He spun me around and slapped handcuffs on me. As I twisted and kicked with fury, everyone seemed to be screaming at once, including me. The next thing I knew, I was being pushed roughly into the back seat of a patrol car, swearing as the door was slammed shut.

After I quieted down, my brain fog cleared enough that I realized that all our cars were facing the wrong way on what I now saw was an on-ramp, not an off-ramp. I'd been speeding down I-80 *in the wrong direction!*

I could have killed someone, I thought guiltily, deeply shaken at the realization. *Or myself. But that would be no loss,* I added, finishing the morbid thought.

What happened next is a blur. The only other thing I recall clearly about my arrest is that with my hands cuffed behind my back, I couldn't wipe away the tears and the mucus from my nose, and it was running down my face as I was escorted into the police station.

I was held overnight. The old memories of being behind bars in Florida and Georgia flooded my mind once I was locked up.

The next day, after my arraignment and release, I entered my parents' home just as Dad was coming out of the bathroom, newspaper in hand. "Gina," he said after he took a good, long look at me, "next time you make the papers, make me proud of you, not ashamed."

I felt my face burning with shame. I had no idea the incident had made it into the papers. I'd hoped to keep it a secret. (After all, what's one more dirty secret on top of all the others?) But now they all knew—family, neighbors, old friends, the pack. Even people at the Catholic church I'd grown up in, which my parents still attended. Once again, I'd brought more humiliation on myself and my family. I'd also given the pack more ammunition for the future.

*   *   *

It had been nearly a year since Ray had divorced me. My life had spiraled downward in a hurry after that. I was in a rush to numb my pain. It was as if all the dirt of my past had resurfaced and covered me once again, and since I couldn't scrub myself clean enough, I'd tried to wipe out the ugly thoughts and feelings with alcohol. But that wasn't strong enough, so I'd added pills into the mix.

Little wonder I soon lost my job.

I also lost my apartment, but for different reasons. Immediately following the divorce, I stayed in the loft apartment I'd shared with Ray. Ray's family owned the place, however, and it didn't take them long to evict me. Since I didn't have the resources to get a place of my own, I grudgingly moved back into my parents' home. It felt like a huge statement of more defeat and failure. A giant step backward. Here I was, twenty-nine years old and living in my childhood bedroom once again. Where even the walls and furniture held bad memories that taunted me. Could I not do anything on my own without falling on my face? Evidently not.

But maybe this time it will be different at home, I thought. Then I caught my ridiculous thinking. *I'm kidding myself. This home, this family, and how I am seen and treated will never change.* I could not have been more right, but it never occurred to me that I, too, needed to change. I was no angel, and in the years since my escape from being trafficked, my behavior had deteriorated considerably. I'd become guarded in every relationship. Defensive. Quick to anger. Even spiteful. I'd become a fighter rather than the quiet victim of my pretrafficked days. I'd love to excuse that by saying it was because I'd been severely traumatized and hadn't healed. Both are true statements, but that was no license for my poor behavior. Yet I didn't see it at the time. All I saw was that it was me against the world—a cruel and unfair world.

I needed a job, but this time I didn't set my sights as high as school or a respectable office job. I didn't feel worthy of either. Instead, I headed to a bad part of town where I'd been drinking and doing drugs, and I landed a job as a bartender. I'd never been a bartender in my life, but they didn't ask, so I didn't tell. I learned the work quickly. The area was known for shootings and stabbings and prostitution, but I didn't care. I didn't really want to be alive anyway.

As always, I was good with the customers. After all, I could act happy and funny and friendly. I could wear a smile on my face even if I felt like I was dying inside. I'd had plenty of practice when I'd been "in the life." There were lots of regulars at the bar, and it didn't take us long to figure out how to speak a secret language. Soon, rather than cash tips, customers would squeeze their favorite drugs into my hand. Uppers. Downers. Hallucinogens. All washed down with a strong drink. I'd try anything, as long as it took away the pain for a while. But I quickly learned that hallucinogens weren't for me. I had enough real nightmares and images haunting me. I sure didn't need to add any more. Downers were my favorite. They numbed the pain the best.

The time of day had nothing to do with using at all. It could be morning, afternoon, or evening. Sometimes, late at night, if my pills were wearing off and I was starting to get lost in thoughts of my past once again, I'd sneak into my parents' finished basement and steal some of their liquor so I could fall into a stupor and sleep once again.

There were times I would wake up in the hospital, not knowing how I'd gotten there. At least twice I took pills by the handful, hoping to never wake up, but then I'd later find myself in a psych ward. While I felt safe, the hospitals could never help with my core issues. I never mentioned my tortuous past, and the doctors' diagnosis would always be depression. So I would walk out of the hospital in a few days even *more* medicated.

I had slogged through a year of this behavior, hating myself and my life, until the night of "the chase." Spending that night in a holding cell proved to be a wake-up call. Coming home afterward and recognizing that my existence was reduced to sleeping it off in my childhood bedroom with nowhere else to go was intolerable. I looked in the same mirror that had been staring back at me all my life whispering words of worthlessness, fear, and shame. It didn't show me, of course, that I was practically buried under invisible chains. That the weight of them had me almost bent to the floor, restraining me from inching forward in life. No. All that mirror showed me was a broken, nearly thirty-year-old woman with dead eyes, hollow cheeks, and no future who hated her life and was dying for her next drink. I wanted it bad. And that's when I made a decision.

I need help.

Three small words. But they spoke volumes. I realized I couldn't do this on my own.

I spent the next few days thinking and preparing myself and struggling against the urge to get drunk or high until finally one evening when both Mom and Dad were home and I walked into the living room and addressed them.

"I need to talk to you both about something important," I said.

They looked up at me, waiting. I could see dread on my mother's face. Who knows what she was expecting to hear. Dad looked suspicious and skeptical.

"I need help. I've got to stop drinking and using. But I can't do this alone."

They were silent. Mom was fighting tears. Dad was scowling. They looked at each other for a moment, then back at me. Dad finally broke the silence.

"You don't need anyone's help, Gina. You can do this on your own."

And that was the end of the conversation. I look back on that moment and wonder what I was expecting them to do. Whatever it was, they didn't do it. But in that instant, I knew I was seeing things clearly. No matter what my parents thought, I *did* need help. Not from them, though. I needed help from somewhere outside our broken family system. And it was up to me to find it.

I spent the next few days scouring the phone book and making phone calls. (This was 1981, before the internet.) It was exasperating. I kept hitting brick walls and dead ends. No space. No referral. Long waiting lists. Exorbitant fees. At times I almost gave up and grabbed a bottle. Then, finally, a godsend. I found a drug and addiction treatment center in Morristown, New Jersey. They had a twenty-eight-day residential program, and they had a spot for me.

And so a new chase began: my pursuit of sobriety.

• • •

Life-changing. Eye-opening. Mind-boggling. Transformative. Words fall short. What I can say is this: I checked into the treatment center for a twenty-eight-day stay. The professionals decided I needed to stay for six months. There was much work to be done.

A lot of that work revolved around the Twelve Steps of Alcoholics Anonymous (AA), which would, over time, become foundational to my healing journey. These steps were foreign to the way I'd always operated, and nothing about them came easily to me. I'd always felt like I lived in response to others, who seemed in control of everything—from childhood through my captivity to my marriage to Ray to the past year back at my parents' home after my divorce. But to accomplish these twelve steps, I'd have to take responsibility for my own intentions, thoughts, and behaviors.[2] This challenged my assumption that I was always a victim without the freedom to make my own choices. Frankly, the ideas in the steps rattled me. But determined to chase my sobriety, I threw myself into trying to understand and apply them. I cooperated eagerly in group meetings, small groups, and individual counseling.

However, a program, no matter how well structured it is, can take you only as far as you are willing to go. I was honest and earnest in wanting to recover from my addictions. But there was one thing I was not willing to expose—my abduction and years of being trafficked. I never mentioned it. Not in group sessions. Not in private sessions. Not once, to anyone. Not even a whisper. I was developing strong relationships with others in the program and was simply too ashamed of that part of my life to take the risk of losing those people. I see the irony. We were all exposing the worst of ourselves to one another, so why hold back? But the shame went too deep. I'd risked telling my friend, and she'd shut me down. I'd risked telling Ray, and it had cost me my marriage. If those relationships had been unable to bear the weight of my secret, how could any of these new relationships?

I convinced myself that if I ever revealed this toxic secret to anyone else, my relationship with them would be sabotaged. So I decided I would just lock it up, bury it, and throw away the key. I believed that I could mindfully forget that any of it had ever happened. I chose to intentionally bury those nightmarish years so deep within my soul that I'd forget they ever existed. And that's exactly what I did.

When my six months were up, my counselors recommended that rather than move out on my own, I transfer to Mrs. Wilson's

Halfway Home. This halfway house had a terrific reputation, but it was apparently very difficult to get into. However, the timing was perfect, and I was admitted. I lived there for more than a year. There I learned a lot about living a relationally healthy life and overcoming old habits and ways of thinking. I could see my progress and was filled with hope.

Yet I still kept my secrets.

• • •

While at Mrs. Wilson's, I went job hunting and found a nice position at AT&T as a customer-service representative. I enjoyed the job and the sense of purpose and accomplishment it gave me. Things were looking up.

I also decided that if I was going to live out AA's Twelve Steps, I'd better get busy finding out more about God, since He played a major role in most of the steps. So I started attending services at a nearby church. In the past, attending church had been all about the ritual and the mystery and the beauty of the experience. I knew of no other approach to religion. A real, loving God still seemed like a distant idea, and I struggled to understand who He really was. That made church services difficult to comprehend. I often felt like an outsider who didn't know the secret language or secret handshake of an exclusive club. Nevertheless, I continued attending church.

It was at this little church that I met Joe. I discovered through our small talk that he, too, was in recovery. It felt good to have that in common. He was a roofer by trade who now inspected commercial roofing. A good job. Joe was handsome, lighthearted, and funny, and he was very easy to be with. It didn't take us long to realize we felt an attraction to each other, and soon after, we started dating. Interestingly, my counselor and AA mentor cautioned me that forging a romantic relationship at this point with another person in recovery might be fraught with trouble. But it felt so good to see Joe's face light up when he saw me and to laugh together. Besides, Joe really loved God and enjoyed talking about Him. This was a new experience for me. I wanted whatever it was that Joe had.

When my time at Mrs. Wilson's came to a close, I was again advised that I wasn't yet ready for life on my own, so I entered another rehab home and continued to discover what a life of sobriety looked like. I also continued my job and my relationship with Joe. After a year in rehab, I was finally ready to step out on my own. Joe and I decided to move in together. My counselor and my mentor advised against it, but Joe and I were in love and were convinced that this was right for us. So we found a small apartment and made our move.

This marked the beginning of another sort of chase: my pursuit of a family of my own.

I emerged from the three treatment facilities sober and well steeped in the Twelve Steps. I'd grown by leaps and bounds. I'd made significant progress in relinquishing so much of my old, broken thinking. I'd taken my first steps toward new methods of communicating and relating and thinking. I'd even begun to understand that all my life I'd never learned to face my problems and deal with them. Either my voice had been silenced to the point that I was unable or unwilling to admit or address my problems or I'd numbed myself to them. I wanted to break those old patterns. Gone were the feelings of despair. Gone were the thoughts of ending my life. I now wanted to live, fully. I felt loved, and I enjoyed loving Joe.

Yet I *still* kept my secret of having been trafficked. Even from Joe.

• • •

Joe and I had our ups and downs—and that's putting it mildly. On the positive side, we were wonderfully in love and began nurturing each other's dreams of the future. We spoke hopefully of having children together. Joe had been married before and had two children, ages three and five. For all intents and purposes, that made me an instant stepmom, a role I threw myself into with joy when the kids stayed with us on occasional weekends. Since Joe and I had both known the depths of despair in our past struggles with addiction and pain, we were intentional about celebrating good times together. We loved the beach and went often. Joe also loved to fish and taught me to love it as well. He enjoyed grilling, and we both enjoyed entertaining, so we made friends and had them over for barbecues. We laughed *a lot*. I'd never had such a rich and fulfilling relationship in my life.

On the flip side, we were immature at sober living and conflict management, and we carried a lot of baggage from our pasts, so when we argued, we argued big. Ours was a volatile and turbulent relationship where tempers flared too easily, and sadly, at times this led to physical altercations. Yet in spite of our struggles, we both planned to stay together for a lifetime. We were determined to overcome our differences and worked diligently to do so.

Our first two years flew by, and at that point, we decided we wanted to declare lifelong vows. We discussed having a Catholic wedding, but that would have required seeking annulments for our first marriages. Neither of us felt comfortable with that idea. From my perspective, annulment seemed like declaring that those marriages had never been legitimate, like throwing our previous spouses under the bus. That was something I didn't want to do. So in 1985 we married at city hall before a justice of the peace. My parents then hosted a small, intimate dinner at their house a few weeks later. I was thrilled and looked forward to a lifetime with Joe.

Our desire was to have children together, so it was with great joy we discovered that I was expecting. Sadly, I suffered an ectopic pregnancy and required emergency surgery. While I was lying in my hospital bed recovering, a memory I'd tried to bury resurfaced.

I was driving along Route 17, a busy highway, when I noticed a group of people gathered on a sidewalk in front of a nondescript building. Many held signs that made me curious, so I moved to the right lane and slowed down as I passed. I saw the words *baby*, *life*, and *abortion*. I felt compelled to stop and read the signs, so I circled back, pulled over near the protestors, jumped out of my car, and walked up to the group. That's when I saw something I'd never seen before: pictures of a baby in the womb at different stages of pregnancy. When I'd aborted my first pregnancy, I'd been told that what they were removing was "just tissue" and "not a baby yet." But these signs proved otherwise. My stomach suddenly twisted in knots, and my breathing grew erratic. I felt like my heart was screaming. *What? How can this be?* I thought as panic surged through me. *These are babies! Not clumps of tissue.* I looked more closely at the photographs. Little heads, little bodies. Tiny hands and feet. Then I saw pictures of aborted babies on a few signs. I was afraid I might vomit right there. I felt like a bomb was going off in my brain. *These are babies! Babies!* I wanted to scream. *That's not what they told me! Why did they lie to me?* I felt so betrayed.

Deeply shaken, I made my way back to my car and just sat there. Traumatized and shocked, I broke into tears. I was filled with remorse and sadness. And anger not only at others but at myself as well, despite the fact that I'd been told my baby was just tissue. I was mystified. And overcome with guilt. I'd never in my life tuned in to any articles or reports about the battle over abortion. I'd seen it as some political issue, and since I didn't consider myself a political person, I'd ignored it. Now I sat in disbelief at my own naïveté and the deception I'd fallen for. I'd been so young and vulnerable. Oh, how I wished someone had told me that I had options so I would have been able to make a wise, life-giving decision. I felt as if my spirit had been blown to smithereens.

Now, after my emergency surgery, this memory came flooding back. During this period of loss, I wrestled even more with my understanding of God. I feared I was being punished for my abortion—a shame I'd never dealt with. Was this present loss of our baby my fault? I believed it was. I began having nightmares about my abortion.

Months later, I conceived again. This time I understood clearly that there was a living child inside my body. But I miscarried. Was this a curse from God? Surely I deserved it. Another miscarriage followed. My doctor informed me that carrying a child was dangerous for me and that I'd likely never give birth. The grief Joe and I felt was crushing.

But one positive thing came from this experience: Joe and I grieved together and actually grew stronger as we comforted each other. Never before had someone grieved with me over a trauma or loss. It didn't take away the pain—the loss left me with a hole in my heart—but what a miracle it was to feel loved, understood, and comforted in my loss. And how satisfying to offer that same love, understanding, and comfort to Joe.

As we neared our second anniversary, I had a lot to celebrate. I'd been chasing sobriety for about six years and a family of my own for two years, and I'd caught them both. But given my history, I couldn't help but wonder whether they were mine to keep or might slip away. And then came some shocking news: I was once again expecting a baby.

15

INTO THE LIGHT

The people dwelling in darkness have seen a great light,
and for those dwelling in the region and shadow of death,
on them a light has dawned.

MATTHEW 4:16

"YOU'RE NOT GOING TO BELIEVE THIS, GINA," Joe said with amazement as he reentered the delivery room after taking a break in the waiting room for a few minutes. "There are now sixteen members of your family out there!"

"What? You're right. I don't believe you. You're teasing me," I said, laughing. Joe was always joking, and I assumed now that he was just trying to distract me from my labor pains.

"I promise you, Gina. They're everywhere, sitting on chairs, end tables, the floor. It's like a big party out there. Everyone is rooting for you. They're making bets on boy versus girl. Everyone is so excited that you're giving them the first grandchild in about a dozen years."

Another hard contraction came and went. I decided Joe had to be telling the truth. Already overwhelmed with emotion, I started to cry. But they were happy tears. I never would have believed my whole family would turn out for the birth of *my* child. *Me? The black sheep? Unbelievable!*

Joe couldn't stand still. During contractions he was squeezing my hand, wiping my brow, counting breaths. Between contractions he was nervously (yet happily) bouncing around the room.

"Joe, go check on the waiting room again," I said. "You're making me nervous."

He reminded me of Tigger as he bounded out the door. A few minutes later, he was back. "Nineteen, Gina! Nineteen!" Then he bounced back out of the room.

I was in labor for a very long nineteen hours. Once I'd given birth to our baby, Lisa, I could hear them all cheering as Joe ran out of the delivery room and announced, "It's a girl!"

My pregnancy had been challenging and at times scary. Once we'd nearly lost our precious baby. That was followed by months of bed rest. Now I cradled her in my arms. I was totally overwhelmed with the miracle of birth. She was perfect in every way, an answer to my many whispered prayers. At the moment, God seemed more real than He ever had in my life. I felt like He was *blessing* me—a feeling I'd never felt before. And later, when my mom and dad entered the room, each with tears rolling down their cheeks, I actually felt close to them. *Connected.*

This is what family is supposed to feel like.

•   •   •

In the months following Lisa's birth, I knew joy I'd never known before. My parents, siblings, aunts, uncles, cousins, and even various individuals in the pack came to visit, sharing gifts and joy. At family gatherings, Lisa was the star of the show. Whenever Joe and

I walked into my parents' home with Lisa, everyone's faces lit up, and we were welcomed with hugs and kisses. I'd never had such an experience with my family.

At the time of Lisa's birth, Joe and I still lived in our first apartment, about forty-five minutes from my parents' home. During the first year of her life, we spent quite a bit of time driving back and forth to visit my family. By the time a year had gone by, a few things were clear. First, relating to my parents, and even my siblings and the pack, was going well. Second, everyone kept telling us that they wanted to see us more often.

"Let's move closer," I suggested one day. "My family would love to see Lisa more often."

Apart from Joe's two children from his previous marriage, he had no other family connections or obligations in our area, and he was all in favor of the move. We found a place back in my childhood neighborhood that was just a block from my old Catholic church. Still feeling a closeness to God and an interest in learning more about Him since childbirth, I had an impulse to start attending church regularly.

"Let's start going to church there, Joe. We can even walk!" And so we did.

I quickly got involved in the church. They had a social-services ministry that delivered clothing and food to needy families—something I could do with Lisa in the car with me. I still had my job at AT&T, but I could easily serve on weekends or after work. I was all in. We were getting to know people, and Joe and I beamed when they admired Lisa.

One Sunday when I attended Mass without Joe, I stood in line to shake hands with the priest, who was standing, as usual, in the back of the sanctuary greeting people.

After greeting me, he took on a serious expression and said in a quiet voice so as not to be overheard, "Gina, I noticed you received

Communion today. I don't recall ever getting notice that you had your first marriage annulled."

"No, I never followed through with the annulment, Father. Joe and I decided not to."

"Well, you'll not be allowed to receive the sacraments then, Gina. Also, if you don't annul your previous marriage, you can't serve in any of the ministries."

I recoiled as if he'd given me a gut punch. I wanted to explain that Joe and I felt we couldn't in good conscience annul our first marriages, but as I tried to catch my breath and find my words, the next parishioner in line stepped up, and the priest turned to her and shook her hand. And that was that.

I practically ran the one block home and burst through the doorway crying. I felt as if I'd just been rejected by the church. *My* church. My family's church. The church of my childhood. Communion still held a special place in my heart. It was the only experience in church that made me feel connected to God. Like Lisa's birth, it gave me an intense sense of God's presence, just as it had my first time. Now, because I was divorced, I wasn't good enough to take His body and His blood? I didn't understand.

Joe was in the kitchen and came running at the sound of my crying. He held me as I sobbed my way through an explanation. Finally he held me at arm's length so he could look into my eyes. "Honey, don't you worry. Do you remember my old friend Jerry, the pastor at that little Nazarene church? He's a good friend, and I know he loves God so much. I've been to his church before, and I think you'll love it. That church will welcome us. We'll go there. You'll see."

I quieted, and we agreed to go the following Sunday.

• • •

I'm not sure what I was expecting when I first stepped into the Nazarene church, but I certainly didn't get it. I was profoundly underwhelmed. Having been raised in an old Catholic church building, I was used to an ornate sanctuary—beautiful stained-glass windows, statues, candles, and a carved wooden altar with a fine altar cloth in front of the huge crucifix. The majesty of the place always made me feel like I needed to whisper. This church building didn't feel like a church at all. It seemed plain and bare, with no stained glass or statues. The pastor didn't even wear a robe or a collar—just a suit and tie. And there was no magnificent organ music. Instead they had a worship team of musicians playing for about half an hour before the service began. *I'll never feel God's presence in this place,* I thought.

Of course, I was carrying with me the sting of feeling rejected by my Catholic church, an experience that intensified my dissatisfaction with everything. It was as if I'd been demoted to what seemed like a second-class church, and it hurt. Joe, on the other hand, seemed right at home, without the uneasy demeanor he'd had at my Catholic church, where he'd always seemed to feel like a fish out of water. But in spite of my misgivings over the physical aspects of this new church, I did appreciate how warmly we were greeted. People came up to us not only to welcome us but to start conversations and actually get to know us as well. I had Lisa in my arms, and she drew all kinds of pleasant attention.

When the service started, we sang a few songs I'd never heard before. For the first several minutes, I was put off by the simplicity of absolutely everything. It took me a little time to stop judging and start listening. Eventually it dawned on me that, unlike at my Catholic church, I could understand everything that was going on here. I appreciated the warm welcome from the pastor and an opening prayer that touched my heart because it was prayed in everyday words. It didn't sound churchy or mysterious at all. It sounded like a simple conversation with God. Tender and fresh. That was new to me. Then came the announcements about a fellowship dinner and Sunday school and youth activities that drew me to these people and their love for their kids. When the pastor read several Bible verses, I loved the way he read them—as if he was speaking to us personally. It was like nothing I'd experienced before.

Then the time came for the sermon, and I was again blown away. Pastor Jerry talked to us about the Scripture passage he'd read, what it meant, how to make sense of it, and how it could influence the way we live. He was so personal in everything he said, and to my amazement, I understood everything that was happening. By the time the sermon was over, I knew I wanted to come back. I didn't need stained glass and statues to feel God's presence after all!

From that time on, going to church together was woven into the fabric of our lives. Sunday mornings evolved from a religious practice to a personal journey of growing closer to God. I did still grieve that I'd lost having a church my family attended, the place where I'd first participated in the sacraments. I felt devastated, as though my spiritual roots had been torn out from under me. But I felt like a new seed for spiritual growth had been planted.

I began to understand that on our spiritual journey as a couple Joe was ahead of me. One of the things that had drawn me to him had been the way he talked about God. Now I got it. Pastor Jerry frequently gave altar calls, and one Sunday I knew I no longer wanted to sit on the sidelines. I stood and stepped forward to the altar. And there I confessed that I was a sinner and accepted Jesus Christ as my Savior, believing that He had died on the cross for my sins and been raised from the dead. I was committing my life to following Jesus as my Lord.

That day I realized I'd only been practicing religion when all along Jesus had been inviting me into a personal relationship with Him. It was as if I'd been living in a shadowy land and now I'd stepped into the light. No longer did I just listen to Pastor Jerry's prayers. I prayed along with him in my heart. No longer was I just curious about the topic of the Sunday sermon. I hung on the words to discover what it meant for me. God was no longer just a mysterious idea, a distant being who was looking to punish me for the bad things I'd done. He was my heavenly Father.

But when it came to understanding what that meant, I had a very long way to go. Though my earthly father had been an excellent provider, he had also been volatile, unpredictable, fearsome, and frequently angry. He'd hurt me many times, physically and emotionally, so God as my heavenly Father was still a mystery to me. As for the idea that His love was unconditional—well, I wasn't sure what that meant on a practical level.

Interestingly, it was around this time that my dad seemed to be mellowing. One day I had a terrible ear infection and was in such pain that I took off from work. I was on the couch when the doorbell rang. It was my father. On a weekday, no less. He walked me back to the couch, tucked me in under my blanket, refreshed my water glass, and then sat at my feet, lifting them onto his lap.

"You know, Gina, when I was a boy, I often got terrible ear infections," he said softly. "I remember the pain. So you just rest here and let me know if you need anything." My dad sat there for a long time, gently patting my leg. Eventually I drifted off to sleep, feeling deeply loved. Loved not only by my earthly father but by my heavenly Father too. Dad's act of love that day helped me see both him and God more clearly.

I often think of the moment when I read these words from 2 Corinthians 1:3-4: "Blessed be the God and Father of our Lord Jesus Christ, the Father of mercies and God of all comfort, who comforts us in all our affliction." The Lord is indeed the God of all comfort!

• • •

As Lisa grew, Joe and I grew as well, in spite of my chains. We grew in maturity, in our faith, and in our relationships with my parents and our friends at church. Lisa thrived at our church—from being cuddled in the arms of loving nursery workers to being loved on and taught in the toddler, preschool, and elementary programs. I got involved in the children's ministries myself and loved being part of that great team. Many people at church became our friends, not only to chat with on Sunday mornings but also to have over for dinner, to hang out with on Friday nights, and to share our ups and downs. We sure loved that little church.

I also grew in my understanding of my parents. Now that I was a parent, I could see how challenging it was, and I came to recognize how difficult it had been for Mom and Dad. Hadn't they just done the best they knew how? I understood that children don't come with directions. And my parents' own childhoods hadn't been easy. They'd had their own struggles to deal with. Seeing their love for Lisa, I better understood that they'd loved me, too, but perhaps with the learning disabilities I'd had growing up, they'd been unequipped to deal with me in positive ways, especially since they'd had five children to parent at once. What was important to me now in my late thirties, and later in my forties, was to build and maintain the best relationship I could with my family. I needed to make the most of Dad's mellowing years and Mom's desire to enjoy being Lisa's grandmother and feeding her family at celebrations. I'd spent my teens and twenties trying to escape my family. I'd spent my early thirties trying to recover from the unhealthy ways I'd coped with my upbringing—drinking and doing drugs. Now I wanted to invest myself in being the best mother and daughter and sister I could be.

Then something unexpected happened. Joe's daughter from his first marriage, Julie, came to live with us at the age of ten. Because I loved being a mother, I was excited to now be an active, involved stepmother as well. Julie was a welcome addition. (She wound up staying with us all the way through high school.) Naturally, as in most stepfamily relationships, there were challenges, but Joe and I were committed for the long haul.

Because Joe loved being a dad, we all spent countless hours together cooking, fishing, laughing a lot, and enjoying conversations. We loved our movie nights, our kids' sporting events, and our family vacations at the shore. We felt the same about the Napoleon birthday cakes from the famous Athens Bakery in Teaneck. They were a family tradition Joe started, and we kept it up over the years.

But I don't want to sugarcoat those years. One of the reasons we grew was that we hit some tough challenges. Joe and I had great seasons as husband and wife, but we had some very rough seasons as well. There were struggles, tears, and heartaches along the way, especially because Joe and I came into the marriage with unresolved baggage from our pasts.

And then there was, of course, the pack. One of the women once sent a suggestive letter to Joe offering to have an affair with him and trying to entice him to do so. Joe showed it to me immediately. He was shocked. But it didn't seem to take him long to get over it. I, on the other hand, was furious with the woman and didn't handle the incident well. It stirred up many unresolved issues from my past with the pack. Tempers flared, and ugly words were exchanged.

I knew that God wanted me to forgive her and move on, but

I didn't yet have a mature understanding of forgiveness. I churned and seethed. The fighter in me wanted a confrontation, a duel of words that would leave her humiliated and stripped of self-respect. Fortunately, Joe's more measured response influenced me to lay aside sharp, lethal words. Let her suffer the humiliation of no response, dangling out there in the open, known to the three of us. Because of how interwoven our families were, she continued to be a presence in our lives at holidays and special events, so an unspoken animosity lived on for years. I confess, it took its toll on me. I knew myself well enough to recognize the difference between my response and real forgiveness. Instead of feeling victorious, I felt disappointed in myself.

It's imperative to note that during this season of spiritual awakening and commitment and growth, though I was deeply introspective about my relationships with family, there was an area of my life that remained hidden away in my heart under lock and key: those missing years when I was being trafficked. Back in my recovery years from drugs and alcohol, when I'd buried those trafficking memories and the crippling pain and damage they'd caused, I had truly succeeded in locking them away. I literally had no conscious memories of them when I came to a saving knowledge of Jesus Christ. On the surface, I lived and acted as if those events had never happened. I didn't know it at the time, but it would take years and the work of the Holy Spirit to bring them into the light. However, beneath the surface, in the dark recesses of my heart, the wounds festered and the damage they had caused surfaced in sneaky, camouflaged ways.

For one thing, the wounds continued to eat away at my sense of worth, eroding my hope of personal transformation and growth. I took offense easily. I held grudges and remained bitter and unforgiving on the inside even though I could act forgiving on the outside. I had difficulty trusting people beyond a surface level, which left me feeling detached and lonely even when I was in a crowd or entertaining others. I suspected that others looked down on me. And inside I was a fighter, determined to be proved right in even the most minor disagreements.

Amazingly enough, I was a master at masking all these symptoms so that other people had no idea anything was wrong until I'd either erupt in anger or sink into hopelessness, loneliness, and depression. The result of all this? Even though I believed in the Lord Jesus, my invisible chains were still weighing me down. I was never free of them.

Worthlessness, fear, and shame remained my three constant companions as I kept my secrets buried. I still loathed myself deep inside. I felt like a fake, pretending to be good and kind but actually believing I was deeply flawed. Less than. Never good enough. I was insecure. Embarrassed by my errors, mistakes, and word choices. Afraid my words were never good enough and always wondering if others thought I sounded stupid, as I'd always heard as a child. I lived in fear and constant anxiety about a thousand things. My severe nail biting continued to the point of pain and bleeding. Such thoughts and feelings were always with me. They'd been my companions forever, and I just had to live with them, I assumed. In choosing to continue living a clean and sober life, I refused to numb them with substances. I simply endured them. I knew no other way. But through it all in this period of my life, I didn't consciously link this suffering with my abduction, abuse, and forced prostitution. Those memories were too well buried.

· · ·

Another challenge was that Joe suffered from some serious back problems in his forties, which eventually required two back surgeries. This hit us hard financially, since Joe couldn't work. I needed to take on a second job in addition to caring for him and the girls. It left Joe and me stretched to our limits.

By the time 1998 rolled around, we were both emotionally fatigued from enduring one rough season after another. It occurred to me that Joe's fiftieth birthday was approaching. I was forty-six at the time, and I was beyond grateful for our years together as husband and wife and parents of Lisa and Julia. I decided to throw him a fiftieth birthday party, the likes of which he'd never had. With a long guest list. A feast to behold. Special music. The sharing of great stories. Decorations galore. I wanted to celebrate this man, and I threw myself into the preparations. By all appearances, Joe loved it, and it seemed to strike up a fresh spark between us for a brief time.

That's when a new loss hit me—a deep loss that ran to the very core of my being. My dad grew gravely ill to the point that the doctor announced, "He's not going to make it." The little girl inside me felt panicked, desperate to hold on to him. I spent untold hours visiting him. I reminisced about the old days, when he'd taken me to his shops. I ached to forget the painful memories of abuse, of my calling the police about the violence in our home, of his disapproval during my teen years. But then I remembered Dad walking me down the aisle and giving me away at my first wedding. My dad was, I realized, a complex man. I felt like he had the heart of a king wrapped in a rough, emotionally volatile body.

As the end drew near, I was sitting by his side one afternoon, just the two of us.

"Gina," he choked out, "it broke my heart when you left the Catholic church. Please come back. Please."

I took his hand and thought for a long moment. Finally I

found the words to say. "Dad, the priest pulled me aside one day and told me I couldn't receive Communion anymore because I wouldn't annul my marriage to Ray. You know what Communion means to you and to me. But I could not in good conscience have my first marriage annulled. But then Joe took me to the church we attend now, and it was there I found the Lord. I asked Him into my heart as my personal Savior. So even though I'm not Catholic anymore, you can be certain that I have God in my heart. You and I will be in heaven together." I squeezed his hand, and he squeezed mine back. It was the most important and personal conversation we ever shared, and it turned out to be the final one we had on this earth.

As our family buried Dad, I found great comfort in the certainty that he and I had an eternity ahead of us. What I didn't know was that around the time of my father's death, a midlife crisis was brewing in my husband's heart. That crisis came to a head in 1999 when Joe, with no advance warning that I was able to perceive, packed his things and left me and Lisa.

My world grew dark.

My heart felt empty.

The Light of the World who had called me into a personal relationship with Him was still there. Yes, I knew that. But I felt myself drifting further and further away from Him.

I felt alone in a dark world.

16

THE DIMLY LIT MIRROR

Now we see in a mirror dimly, but then face to face.
Now I know in part; then I shall know fully, even as I have been fully known.

1 CORINTHIANS 13:12

"I HAVE A SURPRISE FOR YOU, LISA," I said one night as we finished dinner. It was still 1999, and we were finding it difficult to adjust to life without Joe. We missed him terribly.

Lisa was twelve at the time. One of the personality traits I enjoyed so much in her was her exuberance over good news. Joe's departure had hit us both hard, so I'd planned a special night, maybe as much to enjoy her presence as to bring her joy. God, however, had bigger, more far-reaching plans for us than that.

"I know the high school is performing the musical *Annie* this weekend," I said. "Let's go together. And you can bring a friend, too!"

Lisa's squeals did not disappoint, and she threw her arms around my neck. We had a spectacular time together.

As Lisa matured into her teen years, our relationship, to my constant delight, continued to deepen. It seemed that we both had a built-in sense of how to nurture our mother-daughter relationship and a desire to do just that.

I wish I could say that experiencing that closeness with my daughter stimulated me to nurture my relationship with God. But it didn't. Just the opposite was true. I was squeezing God into a smaller and smaller part of my life in those days. Not deliberately, but by omission.

And a relationship that goes unattended has a tendency to shrink.

• • •

Meanwhile, Joe, who deeply loved his kids, understood that relationships need to be nurtured. Though he was separated from me, living in Florida now, and traveling extensively for work, he kept in regular contact with Lisa and with his kids.

One day in 2005, while Joe was in town to visit Lisa (who still lived with me), he had a heart attack that nearly took his life. Lisa and I both rushed to his side at the hospital, where we learned that he needed quadruple bypass surgery.

The doctor told us, "If he makes it out of the hospital, he's going to need rehab here for six months. He'll need a place nearby to stay."

"Mom, Daddy has no place to go," Lisa pleaded.

"Gina, I need a place to stay," Joe said.

"Okay, you can stay with me for six months," I replied.

So I rearranged the lower level of my house to carve out a living space for Joe, with the plan that for the next six months, Lisa and I would care for him. But as is often the case, even the best-laid plans are disrupted. Joe's bypass went well, but while recuperating at my home, he injured his shoulder and required rotator-cuff surgery and then more rehab. Then he had a second heart attack and even more rehab. All in all, Joe's brief visit turned into a two-year stay.

The good news is that they were two good years. Tough in some ways, but good. Seeing each other on a daily basis, yet not viewing one another as husband or wife, nudged me into a new way of relating to Joe. My understanding of him grew. I was able to witness and appreciate the strengths that had drawn me into loving him, without expecting him to meet my needs. I was also able to value and affirm his love for Lisa, which was so very important to both of us. Remarkably, as I witnessed his shortcomings and his needs, I no longer tried to fix or change them. I moved into a much healthier place of accepting the real Joe.

Fully recovered, Joe departed in 2007. But I'm grateful that we parted as special friends with a lifelong connection and a solid sense of wanting to do our best to coparent Lisa in a healthy way for the rest of our lives.

We proceeded from there to an official and cooperative divorce. All in all, from the start of our relationship in 1983 to finalizing our divorce in 2008, I will always be grateful that God gave me a beloved husband of twenty-three years, an incredible daughter when I supposedly couldn't bear a child, and an introduction to the church where I heard the complete gospel and accepted Jesus Christ as my Lord and Savior.

But now, after the divorce, my relationship with Jesus was no longer on my priority list. God was still important in my life, but not as central as He had been when Lisa was a baby.

• • •

In addition to the divorce in 2008, three other circumstances reshaped my life in significant ways. Each of them could have been a powerful motivation to seek the Lord's help and wisdom on a daily basis. But I relied, instead, on my own instincts and muddled through.

First, Lisa met a young man who captured her heart, and that relationship was growing more serious. Of course, Lisa's happiness meant the world to me. She'd been the biggest blessing in my life. Then why, I asked myself, was I struggling not only with her new relationship but also with her blossoming independence?

I should be celebrating with her, I chided myself. *What's wrong with me?*

Fortunately, the bond I shared with Lisa was strong, so overall we weathered this season satisfactorily. But it took me some time to fully realize just how dependent I was on my daughter, who was now twenty-one. I depended on her as if she were my partner and confidante. I was grieving the need to let go. The time had come for me to adjust to an empty nest—but I loved feathering my nest for Lisa.

I believe one of the reasons I so valued the rich, positive relationship Lisa and I shared is that my relationship with my own mother had often been distant and detached. I'd ached for so many years for a deeper bond with my mother, but I never fully experienced it. I didn't want to lose the bond with the daughter I loved so much. Would her new relationship and her growing independence undo this treasured bond?

Another reason this adjustment to the changes in Lisa's life felt so scary is that she was the only key relationship that had stood the test of time. I had tragically lost every other intimately connected relationship in my life. She was my one and only constant! Was I going to lose her, too? The very idea frightened me. I look back at 2008 as the year these questions surfaced and I wrestled through the answers. It didn't help that this challenge was hitting just as Joe's earlier decision to leave was finalized in divorce.

Ironically, during this time, a woman from among the group

of my abusers had a falling-out with the rest of the group. She'd moved overseas for a few years, and that had angered her friends. Now she needed to return to the States, but she lacked a place to live and the financial resources to secure one. Out of desperation, she reached out to me. Since Joe had left and I had space, I welcomed her to live with me until she could get on her feet.

But I refused to be bullied by the same group that had bullied me as a child. Their bullying hung like a dark shadow over my entire life, so I stuck with my offer, and the woman moved in. After a few months, she was able to move on and eventually mended fences with the rest of my abusers. That's when they retaliated against me. As I mentioned earlier, this group was deeply entwined with my family, often in my home while I was growing up and present at holidays and special celebrations.

In the midst of dealing with this group from my past and working through my changing relationship with Lisa, another major circumstance arose: My mother became seriously ill. She was in her eighties, and her health was clearly declining. I loved my mother dearly, and I had hoped that I could someday draw nearer to her just as I had with my father. I wanted trust, connection, and closure with her.

My abusers, however, had always had close bonds with my mother, so they informed Mom's caretakers that I was not allowed to see her. Beside myself with fear, anger, and panic, I came unglued. When I showed up at the place where my mother was staying, someone called the police. Then one of the relatives denied me and several other relatives visits with my mother. I tried pleading, begging, and demanding. All without success. I even asked a deacon from my church to reach out, but even though my mother wanted to see me and the other banned relatives, he hit a brick wall with those who controlled her care. All this while Mom's health was rapidly declining. Lisa was denied access as well, and she, too, was deeply hurt. It must have hurt my mother, too, because she and Lisa were very close.

Finally, one afternoon, Lisa and I each got a call from a member of the family. "You can see your mother today."

I dropped everything and tore over to see her, arriving in less than fifteen minutes. A caretaker let me in, took me to her bedside, then left us alone. Mom's eyes were closed, but I couldn't wait for her to wake up.

"Mom! Mom! It's Gina. I'm so happy to see you!" I said.

As I was talking, one of the caretakers walked in behind me and put her hand on my shoulder. "Hon, I'm so sorry, but your mother is gone. The funeral home people are here for her now."

I was stunned beyond words. Beyond comprehension.

I reached out and touched her hand. It was cold and stiff. Clearly, my mother had been gone for a few hours. Lisa and I had been called *after* she died. They had ensured that I would not see my mother in her dying days or even her final moments. They'd given me the impression that she was still alive, so I would rush to her bedside, only to find that she was gone. I'd been deliberately and cruelly misled. I could come to no other conclusion.

In this horrendous act of the pack, I'd been abused once more. Just as one of them molested me as a child. Just as they'd physically attacked and beaten me as a child and a teenager. Just as they'd mocked and jeered at me privately and publicly. Once again, they had singled me out to be victimized. I'd been cheated out of a sacred deathbed visit with my own mother. This vile act so deeply violated my spirit that I felt as if I'd been emotionally and spiritually raped.

And rape was something I knew all too well.

I fell into a deep depression. For months I couldn't function. I didn't even want to live. I didn't open the door for anyone. Apart from going to work, I stayed secluded. I lost my job. A friend of mine kept leaving devotional materials at my door. People tried reaching me by phone and through the mail and at my door, but I would not respond. I just felt like everything—everyone—close to me had been taken away.

• • •

As 2009 dawned, I was slowly recovering from all the trauma and loss of the previous year. On my own, I started taking the tiniest of steps of opening myself back up to the world. I steered clear of any challenging relationships but started connecting once again with a few close friends. Each month I took more baby steps. By springtime, one good friend wanted to do something to help me heal.

"You need some companionship," she said.

"I just need to be by myself and get whole," I answered.

"I'm going to create a page for you on a dating website," she said.

I remembered an old news story about people meeting each other online and getting hurt, so I wasn't a fan of the idea, but evidently I didn't say no firmly enough. Not long afterward, she told me she'd posted my picture and personal information on the site.

"Look, just go out on a couple of dates. Just a couple."

Hesitantly I agreed.

The first guy I met in a public place. It was about four in the afternoon, and he was telling me all about the cars in his garage and his home and everything he owned. As he talked about his possessions, I was wondering when he was going to tell me something about himself. I also noticed that he was having one drink after another and found myself thinking, *Well, this guy would have me right back in recovery.*

I had prearranged with my girlfriend to call me early into the date and tell me there was an emergency. That way I'd have a reason to leave if things weren't going well.

After she called, I said, "Oh my. I have to get home to my daughter." And that was the end of date number one.

My second date didn't show up where we were supposed to meet. Then when we finally met up, he looked nothing like the picture he posted, so I assumed I couldn't trust him.

I went home and called my girlfriend. "Take me off this site. I'm done."

She said, "Please, just one more. Give it at least three chances."

"Okay. Three," I said. "Three strikes and you're out."

The third guy's name was Peter. I put off a face-to-face meeting with him for more than a month because I was reluctant. I figured he'd be like the other two, but it turned out he was beyond anything I could ever have imagined. The kind of person who makes you think, *Guys like this really don't exist. He's too good to be true. There must be something wrong with him, but I can't tell what it is.* Then after our third date, I was thinking, *He's amazing!*

Unlike the other dates, Peter and I talked about our faith. He was a strong Christian who enjoyed worshiping in the Catholic church because he appreciated having Communion every week. He talked about having a personal relationship with Jesus and about the importance of prayer in his life. I was struck by his humility, his transparency, and his kindness. I explained my Catholic upbringing but said, "It's very important to me that I can understand the message and everything in the service. I want to come away thinking about the message and growing from it. The more we talked about matters of faith and our love for our families, the more we were drawn to each other. And so began a remarkable, rich relationship. As weeks went by, then months, our conversations grew deeper, our laughter grew warmer, and our desire to spend time together grew more important. I fell in love with Peter and was amazed to find myself floating on cloud nine all the time!

Peter and I married in 2012. He met Joe early on because Joe would come to visit Lisa and share special occasions with us, and soon Peter and Joe became good friends. With Peter's support and understanding, Joe and I were able to discover true forgiveness and find real peace in our relationship. I saw Peter as a gift from God, but even with that great gift, I still left God on the back burner during this period of my life. I was only vaguely aware of the distance I'd allowed to grow between us. I certainly still believed in God, but my passion for Him had fallen flat, and I'd become quite passive about nurturing my spiritual life. Yet I didn't see this as a problem I needed to address. I felt quite content to just let it be.

• • •

After my marriage to Joe ended, the challenges of the years that followed left me spiritually lifeless and numb. I did sometimes go to church and tune into the messages, but I rarely spent dedicated time praying or seeking God's will. Due to my lifelong learning disabilities in reading and comprehending information, I rarely read God's Word.

I was used to thinking of my life as a series of disappointments, with occasional escapes from the pain. I had internalized the idea that I'd always been and would always be a victim. It was my normal. My always. I'd never lived any other way. I was completely absorbed in dragging my invisible chains through every life incident I encountered, taking on new links with every sad episode that came my way.

My lifelong belief that I was worthless had convinced me that life would never get richer or fuller or better. Bound by fear, which had been my constant companion from the beginning, I was always on guard, sure that whatever was around the corner was going to hurt me even more. And the shame I lived in made certain I kept my secrets. I turned to no one for help—I didn't deserve it and wouldn't find it even if I tried. I'd never told Joe—my husband of twenty-three years—about the trafficking, so I certainly didn't tell Peter. Tell him what? I'd buried my past so deep for so long that I'd forgotten what my secrets even were. The pack, of course, thought they knew my secrets based on what little they'd heard some forty years ago, but they knew nothing. They had the story all wrong. They pictured me as choosing and enjoying life as a prostitute, making a living by selling my body for a price. And it seemed they thought their job was to make me pay for it in some way.

What I realize now is that I didn't yet grasp that God works with the long range in mind. He always has an eternal perspective as He ushers us through the chapters of our lives. He has a purpose for each one of us. And He has a plan for unfolding that purpose. Had I been reading and studying my Bible and seeking God's heart in prayer, I would have known more about that eternal perspective. But I hadn't been living close to God.

I didn't stop to wonder, *What if God has a grand plan that I just don't see yet? What might it be like to see my life from His perspective rather than my own? What if He has a purpose and a plan for me?* Now, those questions are worth pondering!

But I was pondering my woes rather than God's ways.

And that's how I lived, right up until the fall of 2016 when I showed up at church to serve coffee for the people attending the new Redemption & Recovery program. The night I came away shaken, remembering horrific events from my past. Right up until I sat face to face with Peter, ready to break my silence and tell him my secrets.

Part 6

FREEDOM

2016–Present

17

BOUGHT
AT A GREAT PRICE

You were bought with a price. So glorify God in your body.
1 CORINTHIANS 6:20

AFTER A FEW HOURS OF TELLING PETER my secret story, I had run out of words and tears and finally grew quiet and still. I lifted my gaze to meet Peter's eyes, red-rimmed and moist with the tears he'd been shedding as he'd listened. While I'd been pouring out my heart to Peter on this Saturday morning, he had moved from his chair onto the couch next to me. His right hand was gently stroking my back, his left hand was resting on my leg, and his body was pressed against my side. All this told me that he was fully *with* me, drawn to me as he heard my darkest secrets. Such a picture of love—exactly the picture I needed. I let my eyes linger as they caressed his face. All I could see was love.

"Oh my, how long have I been talking?" I said with a slightly embarrassed grin. "And look! I must have used every Kleenex in the house." Used tissues were on my lap, the couch, the floor. "I never even noticed you running to get more." We both chuckled, then Peter stood, pulled me up next to him, and wrapped himself around me in the warmest embrace I'd ever known.

The secrets I'd kept from Peter were now gone.

I'd spoken all of them to him, and with that, the power they'd held over me had melted away. He now knew that the woman he loved had been abducted, brutalized, and forced into prostitution; that I'd been sexually molested and physically abused as a child; that I'd been raped multiple times as a young woman. He knew about the drug and alcohol addictions. He knew all my dark secrets, but he wasn't repelled. He didn't blame me. He didn't tell me it was my fault. That I'd brought it all on myself. That I'd had it coming. That I'd been a stupid fool. That he wanted me gone. Instead, he wrapped himself around me, drew me to his heart, and held me there.

I was safe with Peter.

● ● ●

I floated through the rest of that Saturday filled with relief. Not that I thought my recovery work was done. Far from it. In just the couple of months I'd attended the Redemption & Recovery meetings at my church and begun private sessions with my counselor, I'd realized that I had a ton of work—hard work—ahead of me. But at least I'd taken one huge step toward destroying the power of the secrets I'd kept for decades—for a lifetime, really, including all the childhood experiences that had left me so vulnerable to shame and fear and believing that I was worthless.

I understood now that keeping shameful secrets was like handing over the reins of emotional and spiritual control to the person or persons who had victimized me in the first place. The old saying was true: You are as sick as your secrets. Secrets leave us isolated, disconnected, lonely, and limited to our own resources. They cut us off from seeking help and healing, leaving us to be victimized over and over again. And, as in my case, they can lead to burying the truth so deeply that we keep secrets from ourselves. That is called *denial*, a word I'd already heard repeatedly at R&R and in counseling sessions.

I had so feared telling Peter about my past, but now, in the telling, I discovered a few things. First, I remembered far more of my history as I told my story. I truly had been in denial. Second, I could given Peter the opportunity to demonstrate and express his unconditional love for me—something he relished doing and I craved experiencing. And third, I became more authentic. More real. More honest. I stopped feeling guilty for hiding part of myself from Peter. I even knew in my heart that our marriage had grown stronger by leaps and bounds because I had revealed the truth and Peter had loved me anyway.

Now I couldn't wait to tell Lisa everything, and her husband. And even Joe, my ex-husband. He needed to know, and I wanted him to know. It would explain so much about the unhealthy patterns I'd carried into and throughout our marriage. And my R&R group. I'd barely begun to open up with them. Now that Peter knew, I wasn't afraid of news getting out. I wanted to be a transparent, honest person. And I wanted help. I wanted to be free of the emotional baggage I'd been carrying. I understood now why I'd been learning the importance of overcoming denial. As it says in Jeremiah 6:14, "You can't heal a wound by saying it's not there!" (TLB).

How appropriate that the first R&R workbook was titled *Stepping Out of Denial into God's Grace*. I definitely wanted out of denial. As for God's grace, I knew I didn't have a full understanding of what that really meant in my life. I was hungry to know and experience more.

• • •

When I returned to R&R the following week, I threw myself into the singing during the opening session, listened intently to the testimony, and then rushed into my circle, where I was able to tell my open share group not only that I had revealed my secrets to some of my loved ones but also that each person I'd told had responded beautifully. I explained that I'd felt validated and affirmed and loved unconditionally. They celebrated with me. But they also pointed out that things often don't go that smoothly as we move through recovery and that I should be prepared for both positive and negative responses not only from others but from myself as well. (It was a helpful reality check that would prove true many times over.)

Later that week, I attended a step study, where R&R small groups discuss responses to the homework in the workbook. Since telling Peter my secrets, the workbook had come alive to me. I felt like every question had been written with me in mind. It was uncanny! But the workbook wasn't the only thing coming alive. My Bible was as well. The workbook was filled with Bible verses that were piercing my heart, leaving it wide open for God's truth. I'd never experienced anything like it.

A key principle I was introduced to early in the recovery process now came into play: God's Word is the ultimate truth and authority. I had to admit that although I'd been brought up in a Catholic church and then spent seventeen years in the Nazarene church, I'd never developed the habit or discipline of spending time reading and studying Scripture for myself. Instead, I'd relied on the pastor's sermons to feed me. That was a passive approach. I needed to become active in knowing God's Word.

One day while reading my Bible, I came across a passage that described my situation completely: "Though by this time you ought to be teachers, you need someone to teach you again the basic principles of the oracles of God. You need milk, not solid food, for everyone who lives on milk is unskilled in the word of righteousness, since he is a child" (Hebrews 5:12-13). What an eye-opener!

That's me, I thought, shocked. I took some comfort in the fact that since this was in the Bible, I wasn't the only one in this condition. Though I was a Christian who loved and believed in God, I'd never invested myself in spiritual growth. I didn't even know what it meant to grow in my spiritual life. Though I did sometimes read God's Word, I was unknowingly putting the word of people before the Word of God. I was a spiritual infant, and I'd stayed that way for many years! Now, finally, it was time to grow up.

In R&R we discussed this passage: "If you abide in my word, you are truly my disciples, and you will know the truth, and the truth will set you free" (John 8:31-32). I wanted what Jesus promised: *freedom.* If I didn't want to be a spiritual baby anymore, then I had to become a *disciple* of Jesus. Being a disciple means being a student, a follower. It means work! If I wanted freedom, the way to do that was to abide in God's Word. To stay in it. Read it. Study it. Live in it.

So not only did I start reading my Bible regularly, but I also began looking for how it applied to my life. The exact moments when I experienced breakthroughs are a blur of blessings, but sometime within my first few months in R&R, God opened my eyes to a number of powerful spiritual truths I'd never understood.

Perhaps the most eye-opening was when I came across two verses that spoke to me on such a personal level that I actually gasped. I reread them again and again: "Do you not know that your body is a temple of the Holy Spirit within you, whom you have from God? You are not your own, for you were bought with a price. So glorify God in your body" (1 Corinthians 6:19-20).

No, I really had not yet learned that God's Spirit literally lives in my body. That had never seemed real to me. I'd thought of it more as a figure of speech. But now I knew God's Word truly meant what it said. The Spirit of the living God lives inside my body! As for my body not belonging to me, I fully knew what that was like. My body had belonged to my traffickers for almost three years. They had controlled where I lived, where I slept, and even whether I slept. They determined the name I went by and what I wore, right down to my underwear and my shoes. They decided whether I ate, when I ate, what I ate. They had access to my body any time they wanted for as long as they wanted, to do with whatever they pleased. And they rented my body out to men for the price they negotiated. But the money for my time never came to me. It went to my owners. I often didn't even know what that price was. But I sure knew what it meant to be "bought with a price."

My emotions now churned with new thoughts and feelings. What if I really lived as if *God* owned me? Like God was entitled to all of me, night and day? Like His will was the deciding factor in every decision? I had to admit that I didn't live that way. I lived more like I belonged to *me* and when the mood struck me, I'd tune in to what God wanted for a little while. And if it suited me, I'd serve Him every now and then when it felt good and I could work it into my schedule.

Of course, unlike God, my owners had been selfish and cruel and abusive criminals. They weren't looking out for my best interests at all. What was good for me was never their concern. And they paid nothing for me. They abducted me. They stole me. But

God was a different kind of master. He was driven by love and grace. I was safe with Him. I could trust Him. He had paid the ultimate price for me through the life, death, and resurrection of His Son, Jesus.

Was I willing to consider myself a slave of Jesus? To be used for His purposes? To obey His commands? To live fully for Him?

Yes, I was willing. I knew what it was to belong to the wicked. I also knew what it was to run my own life with no one as my master. Both ways of living had brought me misery and pain. Belonging to God was the best, safest, wisest decision I could make. So I made the decision: *Lord, I belong to You . . . 100 percent. I am Yours. No holding back. Not anymore.*

* * *

I find it hard to describe what a difference it made in my life to come to the full realization that God had bought me at the price of Jesus' life. For me, that was the missing puzzle piece—the secret to understanding what it meant to be redeemed.

In the Gospel of Mark, there is a beautiful scene between Jesus and His disciples. Jesus had just finished preaching in parables to a crowd, and afterward, when He was alone with the disciples, they asked Him about the parables. He replied, "To you has been given the secret of the kingdom of God" (Mark 4:11).

That's exactly how I felt! As if Jesus had pulled me aside and said to me, *Gina, you have been given a great secret of God's Kingdom. You know what it's like to be bought and sold for a price, so you'll understand how I'm using the evil you experienced to reveal this secret to you.*

But there was another passage about secrets that made me nervous: "Nothing is covered up that will not be revealed, or hidden that will not be known. Therefore whatever you have said in the dark shall be heard in the light, and what you have whispered in private rooms shall be proclaimed on the housetops" (Luke 12:2-3). My secrets had plagued me my entire sixty-four years of life. Most of the secrets I had were of the wrong things people had done to me. I'd kept some of those secrets because I felt such deep shame over them, thinking that if others knew, they'd see me as the damaged goods I felt I was. Others I'd kept out of fear of retaliation, because of spoken and implied threats. And some I'd kept out of guilt, thinking I was somehow responsible for what had happened to me. I knew it was time to deal with those secrets.

What would it be like, I wondered, if all those secrets were "proclaimed on the housetops" in broad daylight and everyone knew them? So far, only my counselor and Peter and a few loved ones knew. Was it possible, though, that my victimizers would eventually be exposed? Even the pack? Could they, would they, ever be held accountable? And what would that look like? I wasn't sure. But I'd been learning that that wasn't the point. Recovery was supposed to be about *my* healing, not about my predators being held accountable.

My problem was that I had other secrets too—not about what had been done to me, but about what I wanted done to my predators. I had secret anger and bitterness toward those who had victimized me. Thoughts of revenge and retaliation. A desire to punish those who had wronged me. An unwillingness to forgive. Distrust of others. A suspicious spirit that kept me at arm's length from relationships.

I discovered a verse that shed some light on this problem: "Be sober-minded; be watchful. Your adversary the devil prowls around like a roaring lion, seeking someone to devour" (1 Peter 5:8). I already knew I had enemies in my life who wanted to control or hurt me: the bullies at school; the men who'd raped and molested me when I was trying to find work; Charlie, who'd duped me into moving to Florida; my traffickers; those who'd kept me separated from my mother on her deathbed. But it never occurred to me that I had one enemy with the specific goal of devouring me. Suddenly I understood that all my victimizations weren't unrelated, random attacks by wicked individuals who needed to pay for what they'd done. All the attacks I had suffered were actually a coordinated effort of Satan's to beat me down and keep me from fulfilling my role in God's world. He'd simply used my predators as his tools. That gave me a whole new perspective on the importance of fighting that enemy through a new and vibrant relationship with God.

Amazingly, even though this new spiritual information was coming at me all at once, I wasn't overwhelmed. I was overjoyed! I was surrounded by others on the same journey—the journey to freedom. I didn't know yet how or when or why, but I believed what I was being taught: that God wanted to set me free from *all* my secrets.

But at the same time, I was afraid. I realized just how much darkness was still lurking in my heart. Isaiah 43:1-4 became a great comfort to me as I prepared to go deep into those dark corners:

Thus says the LORD,
he who created you, O Jacob,
    he who formed you, O Israel:
"Fear not, for I have redeemed you;
    I have called you by name, you are mine.
When you pass through the waters, I will be with you;
    and through the rivers, they shall not overwhelm you;
when you walk through fire you shall not be burned,
    and the flame shall not consume you.
For I am the LORD your God,
    the Holy One of Israel, your Savior.
I give Egypt as your ransom,

Cush and Seba in exchange for you. . . .
You are precious in my eyes,
    and honored, and I love you."

I was committed to recovering and willing to follow through as best I could. Fortunately, thanks to the solid teaching at R&R, I knew that spiritual growth was *not* a do-it-yourself project. I had an excellent counselor, R&R mentors, and a sponsor to advise and guide me. And now I also knew that I had the Spirit of the living God inside me. It was a good thing too. I was going to need them all.

18

THE SHATTERING
OF CHAINS

[God] brought them out of darkness and the shadow of death,
and burst their bonds apart.

PSALM 107:14

ANTICIPATION. EXPECTANCY. HOPE. WONDER. These are the words that describe what filled me throughout the fall of 2016, in spite of the fact that I'd never wrestled more with the darkness in my soul or worked harder on self-understanding. I'd spent a lifetime in the shadows of worthlessness, fear, and shame. Now, thanks to R&R, my counseling sessions, and, most of all, God's powerful Word, those three evil forces were on a collision course with light, truth, and freedom. Never in my life had God had my full attention the way He did in those months. I could actually feel myself changing! It was like an earthquake in my soul. Everything was shaking and vibrating and shifting. I knew that as I emerged from this period, nothing would be the way it had been before.

Ephesians 5:13 says that "when anything is exposed by the

light, it becomes visible." And that is exactly what happened when I saw myself in the light of God's Word. Those huge, heavy, invisible chains I'd been dragging around for years without even being aware of them became visible to me. The self-loathing and embarrassment, the belief that I was inept and stupid and useless—all of it became visible. The anger, resentment, self-pity, and swallowed rage. The powerlessness, self-blame, defensiveness, hopelessness, loneliness, and depression. All the chains became clear. I needed to see them to be free of them. I'd dragged them through every phase of my life, never truly seeing and understanding the causes and consequences and ultimately the source of it all. And now these chains and the damage they'd been doing were visible to me.

The chains weren't limited to the filthy cesspool of memories of my past. No. They were still entangled with my heart and spirit, every relationship I had, and every aspect of who I understood myself to be. Though it was horrifying to see it all, it was amazingly enlightening and freeing at the same time, because now I knew that "the LORD sets the prisoners free; the LORD opens the eyes of the blind" (Psalm 146:7-8). Freedom was coming.

I came across a story in the sixteenth chapter of Acts that painted a picture of what I was going through. Here's the background: Paul and Silas were traveling through Philippi preaching about Jesus when a demon-possessed woman started following them. She was a slave whose owners made a lot of money off her fortune-telling. So when Paul cast out the demon, it greatly angered them. They dragged Paul and Silas in front of the rulers in the marketplace and claimed that the two men were promoting customs that were against Roman law.

When the crowd heard these accusations, they joined in the attack, and the rulers had Paul and Silas stripped and beaten with rods. Then the men were thrown into prison, and the jailer was ordered to keep them securely. So he locked them in an inner cell and bound their feet in the stocks.

Reading this story, I knew what Paul and Silas felt like being unjustly stripped and beaten and locked up. That was me in Florida. I remembered the fear and the physical pain as well as the emotional agony. Unlike me, however, Paul and Silas spent their time in the prison praying and singing hymns aloud. The other prisoners were listening.

Then I read verse 26. Even today, it takes my breath away, because it tells what happened to me: "Suddenly there was a great earthquake, so that the foundations of the prison were shaken. And immediately all the doors were opened, and everyone's bonds were unfastened."

Yes, I was experiencing a great earthquake. It was shaking the very foundations of the prison that had been holding me captive for forty years! More than sixty years, actually, as I was addressing issues that had held me prisoner since early childhood. All the locked doors flew open. Imagine the fresh air suddenly pouring in and carrying away the stench of my prison cell. I was now standing in that fresh breeze.

And then what happened to Paul and Silas? Their chains fell off! All of them.

What happened after that is just as thrilling, but my attention at this point in my life was on my own chains. Once coiled all around me, weighing me down to the ground, wrapped around my neck so I couldn't speak, around my thoughts holding in the fear, around my heart so I couldn't fully love, around my relationships so I couldn't fully trust. They'd been crippling me for years, and now they had shattered and fallen off. They no longer had the power to hold me. But because these chains had been invisible to me, and because I'd been unaware of the damage they were causing me and those around me, I needed to untangle these fallen chains.

I needed to see them for what they were and understand the damage they had caused. That meant spending time in counseling and in the R&R small group, with my mentor, and with my brothers and sisters in recovery.

It was important for me to understand the *who*, the *when*, and the *why* of what had befallen me. To understand what had caused me to be such easy prey, so broken and prone to repeating the same destructive patterns time and time again.

The first *who* I needed to identify was myself. What was my true identity? I needed to explore the influences that had shaped my past—my parents and family and the pack—and make certain that my past no longer defined me or determined my present and my future. I also needed to explore forgiveness—what it was, what it wasn't, and how to live in it.

This was a tall order.

The apostle Paul wrote, "For freedom Christ has set us free; stand firm therefore, and do not submit again to a yoke of slavery" (Galatians 5:1). Though the chains that had bound me were now powerless to hold me, I hadn't yet learned how to live like I was free of them. I was living as if they still imprisoned me. The next step toward healing was learning how to stand firm in the freedom Jesus had given me.

I discovered a perfect metaphor for what this journey of healing would look like: It would be like peeling an onion one paper-thin layer at a time. Some layers might peel off in big pieces to reveal the next layer awaiting attention. Some might peel off in tiny flakes, with bits and pieces stubbornly holding on. It would take time and work and persistence and courage, but it would be worth it, because at the core—the sweet core under all those bitter layers—I would find freedom.

• • •

In my earliest days of counseling, I found it challenging to understand that my stresses and frustrations and pain often weren't really about what happened in the present. They were about what had happened in the past and had led to my responses in the present. So when I had a relationship problem, the issue wasn't so much about the present argument but what had led to it. To understand the issue, I had to go way back into the past. What were the root causes? What triggered my responses? Why was I defensive? Why was I insulted? Why was I impatient or stubborn or hurt? I discovered that the answers could often be traced back to my childhood and adolescence, well before I'd been trafficked. As a child or teen, what had made me run? What had made me hide or want to disappear or detach from others? The root causes were often the very things that had made me want to choose alcohol or drugs and eventually want to kill myself. Feeling worthless. Feeling afraid. Feeling ashamed. Over and over those three things. And what had caused those feelings way back in the beginning? *I had been a victim.*

For instance, for lack of experience and knowledge, children assume that life in their homes and families is normal. I had assumed that as well. But my life had not been normal. My fear as a child stemmed from living in a violent, abusive home sprinkled here and there with kindness, which sent off many mixed messages. I needed to learn now that those conditions were not my fault. I truly had been powerless to change them as a child. But I was a child no longer. Today I could choose healthy responses to unhealthy conditions in my past as well as my present. I was no longer a powerless victim. I could look at my circumstances through a new lens rather than the lens of a victim. I could learn to see myself as a decision maker, a circumstance changer, an influencer of others. I no longer had to be afraid.

A simple example, I realized, was when my son-in-law invited me to attend R&R. I'd immediately felt insulted and snapped at him. Why? Fear and feelings of worthlessness. I was afraid he was seeing something in me that was broken and needed fixing. And why was that? Because all throughout my childhood—at home, at school, and with the pack—people had called me names and jeered at me and told me I wasn't enough. I still carried the fear that others would see me this way and that, in truth, I was worthless. So what did I do? I snapped at my son-in-law. I returned what I considered an insult by saying, "Maybe *you* need it."

Through my healing, I learned this phrase: *Hurt people hurt people.* How true that was. Because I carried hurt, I inflicted it on others. I also learned the phrase *If you don't heal from what hurt you, you will bleed on others who didn't cut you.* I was living proof of that.

And so my counselor and I set out to face every painful event of my past, peeling that onion layer by layer to find my identity, the truth, and my freedom. It was an agonizing process, but I was deeply motivated because I believed that getting to the core would be sweet.

• • •

When I began to work with my counselor on understanding my true identity, square one turned out to be what I had already learned about being "bought with a price." Jesus had already declared my worth. To Him, I was worth dying for. I was priceless to the God of the universe. I'd already been redeemed! I belonged to God. He was my Savior. I was precious to Him. He loved me. In other words, I wasn't worthless after all! No matter what others might say. No matter what lies I had believed. I was precious to the God who made the universe!

He alone had created me just as He'd intended, and God doesn't make mistakes. So I was not useless or stupid. He'd made me for a purpose, and so I was worthwhile, and with His help, I was capable of carrying out that purpose. I was clueless as to what that purpose might be, but with the help of my counselor, I was learning to see myself through a new lens: as priceless and created for a purpose and dearly loved by my heavenly Father. I had also learned that Peter and Lisa loved me unconditionally, because they knew my entire story and loved me anyway.

One challenge I faced in seeing myself through this new lens was dealing with the memories of being raped and prostituted. When someone is raped, everything is taken. Their mind and physical, emotional, and spiritual well-being. Every single part of them is stripped away. If they're already struggling with identity issues, the theft of their identity is further magnified. In the case of trafficking, they are even given a new name—as if you have ceased to exist.

But believing you have ceased to be you is believing a lie. I needed to come to understand that even though I'd been victimized, my value hadn't changed. I'd spent so many years believing I was who my predators said I was—stupid, unneeded, unimportant, a failure, retarded—that I hadn't recognized the damage this was doing to me. I'd just accepted everything they'd said about me as the truth. Now I got it. I finally understood that continuing to believe all those false claims about my identity was allowing my past abusers to continue victimizing me.

Now I needed to work at growing beyond being a victim to becoming a *survivor*. A victim is someone who suffers harm from the misdeeds of others, while a survivor thrives and grows in spite of being victimized in the past. Frankly, I didn't yet comprehend this concept, but I was assured that I would come to understand it in due time. I even prayed, *Lord, please let me meet a survivor of trafficking one day.*

• • •

Once I had at least an introductory understanding of my true identity and the fact that it had been severely damaged because I'd been victimized, I needed to make a decision: Would I allow that victimization to continue holding me in its grip? If my answer was no, then I had to learn to recognize the ways I was still giving control to those who had victimized me in the past.

Slowly I began to understand my broken behaviors. The self-loathing, embarrassment, and belief that I was inept and stupid and useless. The anger, resentment, bitterness, self-pity, and swallowed rage. The voicelessness, self-blame, self-recrimination, and defensiveness. The detachment, isolation, hopelessness, loneliness, and depression. All these broken responses and behaviors were giving the victimizers of my past the power to ruin my present. I needed to learn to recognize these behaviors as a red flag and remind myself that since God had shattered my chains, I was actually free to choose a new, healthy response to my circumstances, whether or not I felt like I was free. A response that reflected my *true* identity.

This was a lot to take in. And even once I understood the idea, I found it hard to see myself any differently than I always had or to behave any differently. Of all the concepts I'd learned about in all the workbooks at R&R, the most difficult idea for me to apply was finding my identity in who God said I was rather than in who other people said I was.

One day my counselor asked, "Gina, as you look at your past, what was your driving force? What motivated you?"

I knew the answer immediately. My driving force and motivation had always been to ultimately win the love and acceptance of my family. To prove myself. I needed my family to love and accept me. And second, I needed others to accept me as well. I had always found my identity in what others thought of me. If other people said, "Wow, you look so pretty today," or "You're awesome," then I was pretty and awesome. But if someone said, "You're stupid," that's what I was.

Every part of me, every fiber of my being, from childhood throughout my adult life wasn't really mine. I had given myself away to others to do with as they wished, because I was driven to please in order to be accepted and loved. How tragically ironic that I wound up trapped in forced prostitution, where I literally had to do what others wished in order to survive. And, when free of that, I floundered through one failed relationship after another in search of the love and acceptance I could never seem to find.

How was I to find my identity in Jesus when, practically speaking, other people's opinions were my GPS? The secret to claiming my true identity as a priceless child of God, beloved and cared for and created for a purpose, was to choose a new GPS—the Word of God. By knowing and trusting what God has said, I could come to truly believe that He loved and accepted me, no matter what. He proved that on the cross. Then He went a step further and rose from the grave, conquering death. And He promises the same for me: that my soul will live in eternity with Him. That is called *grace*. The gift of undeserved love, freely given to me for nothing in return.

•   •   •

Paul and Silas had experienced that grace themselves, and they were so certain of it and so grateful for it, they were willing to risk life and limb to share that good news with others. In fact, they went even further. When their prison doors flew open and their chains shattered, they could have taken off running. (Like I did the day I discovered that the front door of the suburban house where I'd been held a prisoner for many months was unlocked.) But they stayed put. Why? Because they had a purpose! They wanted to share the truth of eternal life with the jailer and his family. That would have been like staying in my prison waiting for my abductor to come home so I could share the gospel with him. No way would I have done that!

We must remember that the jailer had been told that if the prisoners escaped, he'd be put to death. Here's what happened:

> When the jailer woke and saw that the prison doors were open, he drew his sword and was about to kill himself, supposing that the prisoners had escaped. But Paul cried with a loud voice, "Do not harm yourself, for we are all here." And the jailer called for lights and rushed in, and trembling with fear he fell down before Paul and Silas. Then he brought them out and said, "Sirs, what must I do to be saved?" And they said, "Believe in the Lord Jesus, and you will be saved, you and your household." And they spoke the word of the Lord to him and to all who were in his house. And he took them the same hour of the night and washed their wounds; and he was baptized at once, he and all his family. Then he brought them up into his house and set food before them. And he rejoiced along with his entire household that he had believed in God.
>
> ACTS 16:27-34

Whoa! The decision of Paul and Silas to live out their purpose resulted in the salvation of the jailer and his entire family. I thought back to my purpose: to win the approval and love and acceptance of others. A purpose I would never fulfill.

What must it be like, I wondered, *to have a driving purpose as life-changing and even world-changing as Paul and Silas had?*

I was about to find out.

19

WHAT YOU MEANT
FOR EVIL

We know that for those who love God all things work together for good,
for those who are called according to his purpose.

ROMANS 8:28

ONE EVENING AFTER DINNER WITH PETER, in late 2016,
I was scrolling through Facebook and noticed a post by a lady who
went to my church. She was encouraging people to be aware of
international human trafficking, which was becoming a common
idea in our culture. It was also spotlighted in a variety of ways
through movies, television, and social media at the time.

Intrigued by her interest in this subject, I wrote to her and said,
"A close friend of mine was taken into human trafficking, but it
happened right here in the States." She wrote back and thanked
me, admitting that she hadn't been aware that this was happening
in the States as well. Afterward, I was glad I'd written but felt bad
for not telling her that I was referring to my own experience. The
lie was a red flag that I was still working through my shame.

Several weeks later, I happened to be sitting in church right behind her when, to my utter amazement, the pastor mentioned the New Jersey Coalition Against Human Trafficking during the sermon.

What? My heart skipped a beat. *There is actually a New Jersey organization for this? How have I never heard of it? There's an organization where people actually talk about this? I have to find out more!*

When the service ended, I approached the woman. "Could I talk with you for a minute?" I asked. She nodded.

"I really need to apologize to you," I continued, my heart pounding, "because I wrote to you about a friend of mine who was involved in human trafficking here in the States. I just want you to know that I was talking about myself, and I'm uncomfortable that I lied to you about that."

I was grateful when she responded warmly, and the two of us went on to talk about the New Jersey Coalition Against Human Trafficking (NJCAHT). Then she gave me the name of a woman involved in the organization. I reached out to this woman, and a few weeks later, I sat in stunned silence at one of their coalition meetings. Never in my life had I understood how far-reaching trafficking is or that there is an organization of local people trying to stop it. After the meeting, one of the members approached me to ask how I'd learned of them and what had brought me there. She worked for Villa Walsh Academy, a private girls' school in Morristown. Though I hadn't yet spoken of my experience beyond my immediate family, my counselor, and my R&R group, I found myself spilling out a brief version of my wretched experience.

"Gina," she said, "would you be willing to speak at our school and tell us your story?"

I heard myself agreeing immediately. Me? Public speaking? I'd never done such a thing in my life! But too late for second thoughts.

A few weeks later, there I stood with knocking knees and a dry mouth but somehow eagerly telling the story of my abduction, my captivity, and my escape. The response was overwhelming. Many came forward to thank me for helping them see how real and local the issue of trafficking is and for making it personal and urgent for them. A few invitations followed to tell my story at other events.

If I can raise awareness that might prevent even one person from falling into the hands of a trafficker, I thought, *it's worth it.*

Meanwhile, 2017 arrived, and I continued my counseling and involvement in R&R, which was a one-year commitment that included going through four workbooks. Peter was such an incredible support to me, telling me how very proud he was of my willingness to share my story and do the hard work of counseling and recovery.

By this time, I was the NJCAHT survivor consultant and served on their board of trustees. Through this organization I met several leaders in the fight against trafficking, including Tonya Turner, the president and CEO of UNITAS, an organization that aims to disrupt trafficking by educating schools and helping survivors along their road to healing. I was also invited to attend one of their healing retreats for survivors. I've grown a lot through Tonya's leadership and friendship as we've supported each other's work.

One evening at a coalition meeting, a woman approached me. "Gina, there is a leader in the anti-trafficking movement named Theresa Flores. She would like to meet you." I'd heard of Theresa through her speaking and her books, and I was wide-eyed at her interest in meeting me. She was scheduled to speak in New Jersey soon, and I attended the gathering. Afterward, we spoke.

"Gina, would you like to go on a retreat in Michigan? It's called the Journey of Grace Retreat. Others who've been trafficked will be attending. We're going to meet, we're going to talk, we're going to share, we're going to pray, and we're going to eat together. I'd love to have you join us."

Immediately after we parted, I called Peter and excitedly reported our conversation. "She invited me to go on a Journey of Grace women's retreat . . . and it would help me so much . . . and it would be—"

Peter interrupted. "Absolutely! You must go. Whatever you want to do, yes. No worries."

● ● ●

These retreats were a life changer for me. When I arrived at the first gathering, I looked around the room and remembered my prayer months earlier that I would one day meet another survivor. Now I was surrounded by them. When we shared our stories, I felt an electricity in the air—a deep connection. Sparks flew as we compared experiences, feelings, repercussions, scars, and the struggles of healing. Gina, the outsider, felt for the very first time like an insider. I'd never known such a bond among women.

We slept two or three to a room, and one of my roommates was in her seventies. Our first night, she told me her story of getting into prostitution. It was her thirteenth birthday when her father sold her body to his own brother for the night. Each story was unique, one as sickening as the next, yet we all found common threads. Many stories, like mine, had their roots in unhealthy homes and relationships, where the understanding and expression of love were deeply broken. Learning our true identities and discovering that our pasts did not define us was a journey we all shared. We understood that we were victims, but some, like me, were discovering how to move on from feeling and behaving like victims to growing into thriving survivors working hard not to be held as prisoners of their pasts.

One topic in particular was a hot button for all of us: forgiveness. Some were dead set against even considering forgiving their broken families, or their abusers, or their predators, or the "customers" who'd paid for their bodies. Some felt unable to forgive themselves for their own decisions or vulnerabilities or naiveté or flaws or even for their responses to being trafficked. Some felt angry at the world and the culture that had given birth to such an evil as trafficking, while others felt angry at God for not protecting them or changing their circumstances.

And me? I related to all these forgiveness issues. I was deeply stirred by every story, every hurt, every pain that others shared. I recognized the anger and bitterness in others because the same anger and bitterness were living in me. Clearly, my own journey of forgiveness was only beginning. And I was deeply intrigued by the few among us who seemed to have found some freedom from the ugliness.

When the end of the retreat came (way too soon), I wanted to share it all with Peter. But it was too hard to find words that would do it justice. I finally realized that we victims shared a bond that only other victims could understand and enter into.

. . .

In the late summer of 2017, I came to the end of my one-year commitment to R&R. I had completed all four workbooks. I had grown deeper and wiser and far closer to God. I understood myself and others in ways I'd never imagined possible. But I also understood that I'd only begun to make real progress in knowing my true identity, forgiving myself and my abusers and predators, and growing from victim to survivor. So I signed up for a second year and took the entire R&R course all over again through

2018! I also continued with counseling. I did not want to limp along for the rest of my life as a prisoner of my past.

I thought back to my realization that when I'd decided to fly the coop at the age of nineteen, I didn't know that my wings were broken. Now that I could see how broken my wings truly were—even now—I wanted to learn to fly with broken wings.

Isaiah 40:31 says that "they who wait for the LORD shall renew their strength; they shall mount up with wings like eagles; they shall run and not be weary; they shall walk and not faint." That's what I wanted.

God had so many surprises in store for me. I was working with the NJCAHT as their survivor consultant, and they asked me to review their website and their entire operation, keeping an eye out for ways they were or were not "survivor centered" in their approach. They explained to me that they wanted to become survivor-informed. In 2020, this led to Governor Phil Murphy selecting me to be on the New Jersey Commission on Human Trafficking. This commission is "composed of fifteen members from the fields of law enforcement, victim assistance services, health care and child advocacy, as well as members of the general public who have experience in, or specialized knowledge of, human trafficking." As required by law, one of the commissioners is a survivor of human trafficking.[3]

Meanwhile, when it came to sharing my story publicly through the coalition, I was soaring! By God's grace, I was being invited to share it with college and high school students, medical professionals and law enforcement personnel, parents and educators and lawyers. I spoke to legislators on the House Committee on Foreign Affairs to advocate for stronger anti-trafficking laws. I was invited to be cochair of the New Jersey American Academy Pediatrics task force against human trafficking. I was honored to join the survivor advisory board of Protect All Children from Trafficking (PACT).

It was exhilarating working with these groups to get the word out so that others would not become victims of human trafficking and bringing awareness of how to recognize and help victims. These engagements also helped me make tremendous strides in two personal areas.

First, I now had a deep sense of my own purpose. I believed God was using me, of all people, to help change lives. This was an unbelievable surprise to me. And because my personal story was interwoven with my faith, this allowed me to honor God in all those environments. Surely there was no greater purpose. Second, my sense of identity was healing and growing. I was capable and worthwhile after all, even though I still face challenges with my learning disabilities. Speaking publicly, sharing my faith story, and helping stamp out human trafficking were all part of my newfound identity in Christ. And as that identity grew, God began opening more doors for me to reach out personally to other victims and help them move forward in their healing journeys. This was nothing short of miraculous to me!

Then one day after I'd been invited to speak on the radio about my story, my daughter (who was fantastic at encouraging and affirming me in my new role) ran into a member of my family while shopping. When she stopped to exchange greetings, he surprised her when he said, "Your mother should be ashamed of herself! Doesn't she have any decency? How could she bring such shame on her family by publicly telling these embarrassing stories?"

Lisa was still shaken and hurt when she told me about the encounter. That stirred the flames of my old anger at this family member and my past abusers for all the times they'd heaped shame on me—from the molestation to the physical and verbal abuse to the gossip and lies they'd told about me to the damaged relationships to keeping me from being with my dying mother.

How dare they? I thought.

Sadly, I reacted like a victim, wanting to lash out and return fire. Clearly I still had work to do on the issue of forgiveness.

•   •   •

I'm so grateful to John Baker, author of the four Celebrate Recovery workbooks, for the excellent questions and exercises in *Getting Right with God, Yourself, and Others.*[4] Working through that material a second time, in addition to working hard with my counselor, really helped me put my resentments and lack of forgiveness in perspective. How easy it is to point our fingers at those who wrong us, forgetting that "all have sinned and fall short of the glory of God" (Romans 3:23). And how hard it is to do what Jesus taught us about turning the other cheek and not throwing stones. He said, "Let him who is without sin among you be the first to throw a stone" (John 8:7). It was not my job to cast blame but to live in the grace I'd been given and share that grace with others.

I did discover, however, that it was *not* out of line to *grieve* the wrongs done to me. I found a quote that really brought this home: "Ironically, when we start to get better, we also often get sad—because we start to realize how much we've missed out on, how badly certain people failed us, what the younger version of us actually deserved. Healing involves healthy grieving. No way around it."[5]

How true! I needed to stop stewing, spewing, resenting, and wanting to retaliate for the wrongs others had inflicted on me.

For instance, when I see my daughter, Lisa, today as a mom and watch how she and her husband nurture their kids, it just melts my heart. But I get sad, too, because I think, *Why couldn't I have had any of that as a child?* Take the validation she gives her kids, for example. When they get hurt while misbehaving, instead of disciplining them and focusing on "Who did that?" or "Who was right?" or "Who was wrong?" or whether it was an accident, the first thing Lisa and her husband do is acknowledge the pain and comfort them, soothing the hurt before they talk about it. They're helping their children see their value and worth. Honestly, I didn't get that as a child. So should I resent that and waste a good opportunity to enjoy seeing my daughter thriving as a mom?

Instead, I could acknowledge those wrongs before God, confess to Him that I feel bitter and angry over them, and grieve over the brokenness of it all, recognizing that the enemy is the source of the pain and asking God to give me the grace to extend His forgiveness to those wrongs.

What a difference this made! It enabled me to look at my parents in a whole new light. They were hurt people too. Now I grieved the losses and brokenness in their lives. I always knew that my parents loved all five of us, that there was a beautiful and loving side to each of them. Yes, my mother always seemed detached and distant from me. But at the time I was born, she had tragically lost her own mother. She'd also lost a child before conceiving me. Trying to manage my birth and infancy while balancing the needs of my four older siblings was apparently too much to handle, and she had a nervous breakdown.

Yes, my father had an explosive temper and acted out in abusive ways. But he, too, had been physically abused as a child and had never learned to manage his anger.

Like my own mom and dad, I knew I wasn't a perfect parent but had layers of unresolved issues from my past that seeped into my parenting. I also realized that, though I had good intentions, I, too, had made huge mistakes in parenting that had no doubt caused pain for my daughter and the other children in my care. So rather than resenting my parents, it was time to learn a healthy way to grieve what they and I and my own children had suffered.

Learning how to grieve wrongs was a healthy first step in learning to forgive my parents. The second step was learning to forgive myself and accept God's forgiveness for my sins. I carried so much guilt and shame. I needed to understand the difference between the two. Guilt is a response to wrong behaviors on our part. Guilt says, *You did a bad thing.* Sometimes it is justified because we really did do wrong. That is when we must realize that Jesus died for our sin. His death was enough to cover it all. Our guilt can disappear.

But other times we didn't do anything wrong or bad. The guilt we feel in those moments is *false* guilt, and for that guilt to go away, we must recognize it.

Shame, however, is the false belief that our behaviors or the behaviors of others diminish or destroy our value. Shame says, *You are worth less because of what you did.* But that is simply not true. You are priceless, not worthless! You are loved! Your behavior is sometimes bad (that's true guilt), but you—as a person—are priceless to your Creator.

A third thing that helped me stop refusing to forgive others was learning what forgiveness is *not*. Forgiveness is not easy. We will not always feel like forgiving. It does not mean we must trust someone again. It does not mean "end of discussion." Forgiveness does not mean there won't be any consequences for what others did. It does not excuse or exonerate the other person. And, finally, forgiveness does not make the other person right. Whew! Letting go of those misunderstandings of forgiveness gave me far more freedom to forgive.

The last thing I learned about forgiveness is that it's a journey. It isn't a once-and-done act on our part. It is a process that takes time and must often be repeated. It is a process we must learn and practice over and over again. Forgiveness is a process that is powered not by us but by God. We need God's help to forgive.

I have found two methods that greatly help me when I get

stuck on my journey to forgiveness. One is to write a letter to the perpetrator that I will never send. In the letter, I express my forgiveness for each of the harmful things that person did to me. Here is an example:

> To the family I was born into, the traffickers, and others who traumatized me by inflicting pain, shame, and suffering and treating me inhumanly: Though you've never apologized or held yourselves accountable, because of you I now know my true worth, my strength, and my identity. I know what love is not. You didn't break me. Through God's grace, I have overcome it all and have forgiven you. I have let go.

The other is to write a letter to myself:

> To Gina: You are priceless to the Creator of the world. Nothing you have ever done or ever will do will change that. God chose you to be His child. He created you with a purpose. And because of the death and resurrection of Jesus, when He looks at you He sees a woman who is pure and blameless and beyond reproach. Ask God to help you see yourself that way too.

I would love to say that I have forgiveness mastered. But nothing could be further from the truth. What I can say is that I am committed to *practicing* forgiveness, and I fully expect to *keep practicing* it as long as I live on this side of heaven. There it will be perfected.

In fact, to this day, it seems that several of my old abusers give me the most ongoing practice. Though I've grown much wiser in setting healthy boundaries so that I'm not entwined with toxic people, life circumstances still throw us together. When they do, I might find myself the recipient of the silent treatment, a tongue-lashing, false allegations, gossip, and accusations. I'm learning to see such moments as practice sessions in forgiveness. I am stretching myself to recall God's grace and remember Jesus' example and emulate them both. And when I fail, I lean on God's promise that His grace is sufficient to cover me.

I can say that forgiveness is one of the most healing, releasing, and freeing gifts I could ever have received. The moment I understood forgiveness is when my deepest healing began. Forgiveness put the final seal on the hurtful events in my life. Though I still remember what happened, I am no longer bound by it. Having worked through the feelings and learned what I need to do to strengthen my boundaries, I am much better able to take care of myself in the future.

"Why is it so important to forgive those who are no longer a part of my life?" a friend once asked me. I explained that facing the monster of unforgiveness makes it smaller, so it takes up less space in my life. When I realized this through counseling and my support groups, I was able to truly experience full freedom and pursue my purpose.

● ● ●

If ever there was a Bible story that had the power to correct my lens, or perspective, and give me God's perspective when someone wrongs me, it is the Old Testament story of Joseph. The list of the wrongs Joseph experienced throughout his life is agonizing to read. It started when he was just a kid and his brothers were jealous of the fact that he was his father's favorite son.

When Joseph's father gave him a luxurious, multicolored coat, it only spurred on his brothers' jealousy. After that, God gave him visions of his brothers bowing down to him one day in the future. He shared that vision with them and sent their jealousy over the edge. So they threw him in a pit to die. Then thinking better of that plan, they sold him into slavery. Afterward, they lied to their father, telling him that Joseph was dead. Meanwhile, Joseph's new owners were taking him far away to Egypt.

In Egypt, Joseph was sold to Potiphar, the captain of the guard at Pharaoh's palace. Joseph did such a great job that he eventually became Potiphar's right-hand man. But then Potiphar's wife decided she wanted Joseph to sleep with her. When he refused, she falsely accused Joseph of trying to rape her. As a result of her accusation, Joseph was thrown into prison. He was there for at least two years before Pharaoh summoned him to interpret a dream. Pharaoh was so impressed with Joseph's interpretation that he made Joseph the governor over all Egypt. Joseph was thirty years old at this point. Thanks to Joseph's leadership, the country was prepared when a seven-year famine struck.

Meanwhile, back in Canaan, the famine left Joseph's family without grain. So his brothers traveled to Egypt to buy grain so their families could survive. Of course, they had no idea that Joseph was the governor of Egypt and had oversight of such purchases.

When his brothers appeared before Joseph, he recognized them, but they didn't recognize him. He decided to keep his identity a secret and devised an elaborate plot requiring all but one of them to return to Canaan and bring their youngest brother, Benjamin, to Egypt. When they returned, Joseph continued to keep his identity a secret and fooled them into believing that their youngest brother would become Joseph's slave. They were beside themselves with distress and fear, knowing that if they returned to Canaan without Benjamin, their father's grief would kill him.

Finally, out of compassion for his brothers, Joseph revealed his true identity. Knowing that he had the power to have them put to death, they were terrified. Yet instead of seeking revenge, Joseph spoke words of forgiveness and wisdom to his brothers that should give us all pause: "'Do not fear, for am I in the place of God? As for you, you meant evil against me, but God meant it for good, to bring it about that many people should be kept alive, as they are today. So do not fear; I will provide for you and your little ones.' Thus he comforted them and spoke kindly to them" (Genesis 50:19-21).

What the brothers meant for evil, God meant for good.

In the same way, what my abusers and my traffickers and the pack meant for evil, God could transform into something good. I now recognize that whatever bad things happen to us, God is always at work for our good and His purposes. Our good and God's purposes always go hand in hand. When we fully understand and believe that truth, we see our lives and everything that befalls us from God's perspective, including our part in bringing about His purposes.

20

PRICELESS

God has reserved for his children the priceless gift of eternal life;
it is kept in heaven for you, pure and undefiled,
beyond the reach of change and decay.

1 PETER 1:4, TLB

"GINA, I'M PLEASED TO LET YOU KNOW that we've accepted you into our program," the woman said on the phone. "We're still waiting for the fingerprint and background checks to wrap up, but that's just routine. We'll see you next Monday evening for the first training session."

Yes! I wanted to shout as I waved my hand excitedly in the air to get Peter's attention. But I kept my voice professional. "Thank you so much, Mrs. McCready. I'm really looking forward to getting started!"

I hung up, then turned to Peter. "I'm in, honey!"

"I'm so proud of you, sweetheart," he said, giving me a big hug.

It was 2018, and I was working part-time as the survivor consultant for the human trafficking coalition. I'd also been speaking occasionally as opportunities opened up, so I was already plenty busy. But I'd heard about a need for CASA volunteers, which tugged at my heart. Court Appointed Special Advocates are volunteers who advocate for the best interests of children in the court system who have experienced neglect or abuse. Volunteers work alongside educators and child welfare professionals to make sure that judges have the information they need to make the wisest possible decisions for children's well-being. CASA is a nationwide program, and our local chapter was looking for new volunteers. I knew I could make time in my schedule to serve and was excited at the prospect of helping children, one-on-one, in such practical ways.

I'd been impressed with CASA's selection process. I'd completed a two-and-a-half-hour interview and filled out an extensive application. Next, I'd need to attend some evening training classes for a time and was looking forward to the challenge. The first few classes were fascinating. I took careful notes and knew I'd need to study, since learning still didn't come easily to me. Then on the third Monday, I got an afternoon call from Mrs. McCready.

"Gina, I'm calling to let you know that you don't need to come to class this evening."

"Oh? Is it canceled this week?"

"No, but we received your fingerprint report, and we've learned that you have two criminal convictions on your record. On your application you reported that you've never been convicted of a crime. I'm afraid this means you are out of the program."

"What? Convictions? There must be some mistake!"

When I hung up, my head was spinning. This was insane! I had never been convicted of a crime. My DUIs in New Jersey hadn't resulted in convictions. I'd been arrested once in Florida and then in Atlanta when being trafficked, but I'd never appeared in any court. Could it have anything to do with those arrests forty years ago? I thought all that was behind me. Now I was worried. I had no idea what had come of those cases. I'd been abducted immediately after the first arrest in Florida. And Georgia was where I'd been raped by an officer when I was in custody. There, immediately after my release, Melvin and Candace had forced me into their car and driven out of the state.

Deeply shaken by the call, I sank into a kitchen chair. I felt devastated and afraid. Where was this coming from? And what would happen next? I felt panicked, as if the past were sucking me back in time.

A couple of hours later, Peter saw me sitting in the living room. "Aren't you supposed to be leaving for school?"

"Yeah."

I couldn't process this. I couldn't comprehend it. And I didn't want to tell Peter what I'd heard. That would have made it too real, and I didn't want it to feel real. The old shame and fear were creeping back in. So I grabbed my purse and jacket and left the house. And I wound up someplace I hadn't been in decades. A bar.

After I finished my second strong drink, the bartender offered me a third. I accepted.

I hadn't been a drinker since my recovery days in 1981. On rare social occasions I might have one glass of wine or part of a cocktail, but that was it. All I can say is that I'd been yanked into a state of shock. I couldn't think. I couldn't process. I couldn't problem solve. I felt as if the devil was laughing at me.

"Can I get you another?" The bartender's voice broke the spell. I was hit with a moment of truth. "For freedom Christ has set us free; stand firm therefore, and do not submit again to a yoke of slavery" (Galatians 5:1).

I need to get out of here, I told myself. *I need to get to a safe place where I'm not going to get hurt and I'm not going to hurt anyone else.* And that's what I did. I went home. I sat down and told Peter everything. He, of course, once again embraced me.

The next morning, thankfully, I felt more myself. I called the director of the coalition and told her about the fingerprint report. I wasn't asking for help, just a listening ear.

"Gina, you need a lawyer," she said.

Inwardly I groaned. Worries poured through my mind. *How will I find a good lawyer? Will there be a retainer fee of thousands of dollars? I can't afford an attorney. Can a New Jersey lawyer even help me with cases in Florida and Georgia?*

"I know just the lawyer for you. She's with Volunteer Lawyers for Justice, and she's excellent. She'll get to the bottom of this."

That news was a breakthrough moment. What a godsend! Up to that point, I hadn't even prayed about it. Now I realized that God was providing for me even though I hadn't run to Him as I could have. For some reason, the weight of this shockingly bad news from my past had traumatized me, triggering me to slip into my old victim mindset, chained from head to toe. I needed to behave like a survivor! After all, my shackles had been shattered. So, in prayer, I surrendered the entire situation to the Lord then and there.

The Lord opened the floodgates for me. Shortly after meeting with Jessica from VLFJ, she told me that she was taking my case pro bono! She worked many hours on my case, gathering information and treating me with the utmost dignity and respect. A plan was soon in place. She confirmed that both convictions were for prostitution, the results of my two arrests. Interestingly, I learned that Florida had a vacatur law recognizing that trafficking victims are not responsible for the criminal activity they've been forced to engage in.[6] *That might prove helpful,* I thought. Georgia, however, didn't have such a law. How ironic. I was actually innocent of the Florida charges: All I'd done was accept money from a man I'd thought was a friend who'd offered to pay my airfare for a holiday trip home. It was in Georgia that I'd been forced to prostitute myself.

My lawyer arranged for a lawyer in Florida and another in Georgia to work on my behalf, and they got busy. The reality is, however, that such things take time.

• • •

Over time I began to see that it wasn't such a bad thing to surrender my plans of being a CASA volunteer. God was at work expanding my role in the anti-trafficking movement and revealing His plans and purpose for this season of my life. I was learning how to be an advocate and a change maker, doing research on how other states and countries were (and were not) dealing with trafficking and discovering the dismal realities of what becomes of those who, like me, have been trafficked. Years of abuse, prostitution, drug addiction, arrests, poverty, premature deaths, unhealthy relationships, despair, and suicide are all common outcomes.

That could have been me, I realized. *If it weren't for the Lord and His grace, that could have been my fate.* Safe escapes followed by healthy reentry into productive living were the exception, not the rule.

Meanwhile, I became friends with Theresa Flores and worked alongside her in reaching out to trafficking victims. In fact, I asked her to mentor me in the trafficking fight, and she graciously agreed. One of her initiatives fascinated me. It was called Save Our Adolescents from Prostitution (SOAP). The SOAP initiative targets big events like the Super Bowl, the Indy 500, and the NCAA Final Four. The cities where such events are held are notorious for a sharp increase in sex trafficking surrounding the events. The project distributes millions of bars of soap (free of charge) to hotels and motels in those areas. They label the soap with a red band that prominently displays the National Human Trafficking Hotline number—(888) 373-7888—and they train hotel managers to identify and report human trafficking when they see it in their establishments. It gets results![7]

When it came time for Super Bowl LIV in 2020, I went to Miami Gardens, Florida, to help. There I was, only thirteen miles from Hollywood, Florida, the city where I was first arrested and my trafficking began. I decided to go there and retrace my steps, so I rented a car and off I went. Forty years, I discovered, had brought much change to the area. Old buildings had come down, and new buildings had gone up. I circled around and around looking for Doria's, but it was nowhere to be found. The entire street was now a highway. At first I felt disappointed, but I sensed the Lord saying to me, *It's all gone, Gina. It's all wiped out, just as I've wiped your slate clean.* The Hollywood police station, however, was still there. I parked and walked inside to look around, this time with my head held high, just to show myself that I was no longer a prisoner to those old memories.

Hollywood just happens to be near Miami, where my Florida lawyer's firm was located. I had called ahead and made an appointment. As I stepped into their impressive offices, I realized for the first time that this was truly a high-end law firm. They graciously invited me into a conference room and seated me at a huge conference table. There I was joined by not one, not two, but three attorneys who were working on my case—all at no cost to me. They discussed their findings with me.

"We've been able to locate the report of your arrest, but it's poorly documented. There is so little information in it," one of them said.

"Because the report was so lacking, we took it to the attorney general's office," another added. "They indicated that this case is so poor, it shouldn't even be on your record."

Then the third lawyer announced, "They don't even have any evidence that there was any prostitution going on. We were left scratching our heads, so we hired people on your behalf to investigate this whole case. And that investigation turned up a total lack of evidence. None at all! They can't even find the people mentioned in the report, because there is no documentation on them."

His final words were music to my ears: "We're confident your conviction will be expunged from your record."

I was grateful for such good news.

When it came time for me to leave, the owner of the firm came in. "Mrs. Cavallo, I am so honored to meet you. Thank you for allowing us to help with your case. We feel privileged to be working on your behalf. We look forward to successfully closing your case."

You couldn't even make this stuff up! I just about floated out of the building I was so overcome with gratitude to God. Only God!

While I was writing this book, their vision proved true. Today I hold in my hand the official document from the Circuit Court of Broward County, Florida, dated July 14, 2022, directing the Florida Department of Law Enforcement to "expunge all criminal history records" associated with me. And even more good news: Georgia has now passed a vacatur law, which bodes well for my other case. In addition, I'm thrilled and honored that I was able to give testimony before the New Jersey legislature that has been instrumental in expanding the state's vacatur law.

Yes, everywhere I turn, I see the Lord at work!

* * *

I'll be the first to say, however, that I see the evil at work in this world as well. At times, the stories I've heard from other victims have chilled me to the bone. The ugliness of what one human being is willing to do to another is often too horrific to believe. Yet those stories remind me of what we're fighting for. When I feel myself slipping into heartbreak over what these victims have been through, the following passage of Scripture lifts me up:

> Blessed be the God and Father of our Lord Jesus Christ! According to his great mercy, he has caused us to be born again to a living hope through the resurrection of Jesus Christ from the dead, to an inheritance that is imperishable, undefiled, and unfading, kept in heaven for you, who by God's power are being guarded through faith for a salvation ready to be revealed in the last time. In this you rejoice, though now for a little while, if necessary, you have been grieved by various trials.
>
> I PETER 1:3-6

Yes, the going is rough for a while down here. I see it and feel it too. But God promises that there is wonderful joy ahead. I hold on to that promise!

As I look back over my lifetime, I can now see that even before I believed in Him, God had created and chosen me. He was with me even when the enemy did me harm. God knew from the beginning that He, not the enemy, would win the battle for the life and soul of Gina Cavallo. God was always at work in my circumstances, my mind, and my heart.

He still is. My purpose now is to share my life experiences to help people understand the true reality of human trafficking and create hope for triumphing over horrific crimes against the mind, body, and spirit. I also love educating people about the part they can play in helping survivors experience freedom, healing, and restoration from shame so that we can prevent the victimization of others. Today I live and breathe this! If I can help bring awareness by saving one life, then what happened to me was worth it.

When I'm called upon to speak, I not only share my personal experience as a woman who was abducted by traffickers and forced into prostitution, but I also educate my audiences. This includes law enforcement groups, medical personnel, first responders, educators, faith-based organizations, nonprofit organizations, and governmental agencies, as well as middle school students, high school students, and university students. All these opportunities came to me without any effort to market myself! I wasn't listed with a speaker's agency. I wasn't contacting organizations to promote myself as a speaker. I didn't even have a website until quite recently. I've been astonished as I've watched my platform grow! I know the Lord has opened these doors.

What amazes me even more is how comfortable I am in front of every type of audience. When I'm speaking to children and teens and university students, I look into their faces and feel a driving passion to help protect them from ever becoming victims or to help them heal from whatever abuse they've suffered. I give them the courage to share their pain. I explain that when shame is spoken, it loses its power, and that's when the healing begins.

When I speak to medical professionals and first responders, I pray that the information I share about human trafficking will help them recognize red flags when they encounter patients who might be trapped in trafficking and desperate for someone to intervene.

When I speak to legislators and government officials, I ache to inspire and motivate them to take action, enact legislation, and create policies that will not only help trafficking victims but will also help rid our land of this horrendous blight. A fire burns within me when I step behind a podium and take the microphone in hand.

I was made for this!

I was created for this time and place to be a voice in my culture. This is what the Lord wanted me to see in the words of Joseph: "You meant evil against me, but God meant it for good, to bring it about that many people should be kept alive, as they are today" (Genesis 50:20).

Every single act of evil that was done to me—and that's a very long list!—God is now using for good. Lives are actually being saved and changed—and He is using me to do it. *Me!* The learning-disabled child who didn't even talk until she was five, who failed in school at every turn, who was punched and beaten and molested and humiliated and abused and raped and abducted and addicted! Only God would think of that!

The words of 1 Corinthians 6:20 have sprung to life for me: "You were bought with a price. So glorify God in your body." And Luke 12:2-3: "Nothing is covered up that will not be revealed, or hidden that will not be known. Therefore whatever you have said in the dark shall be heard in the light, and what you have whispered in private rooms shall be proclaimed on the housetops."

One evening after I was honored with an award for my work against trafficking, a young woman came up to congratulate me. I thanked her but assured her that it was God, not me, who was accomplishing great things.

"I don't think you realize," she said, "what an amazing, incredible human being you are and how powerful you are."

I assured her that I realized no such thing and that God alone is incredible and powerful.

As a woman who has struggled my entire life with feeling stupid and worthless and fearful and ashamed, I see my story reflected in the apostle Paul's words in 2 Corinthians 12:9-10: "[The Lord] said to me, 'My grace is sufficient for you, for my power is made perfect in weakness.' Therefore I will boast all the more gladly of my weaknesses, so that the power of Christ may rest upon me. For the sake of Christ, then, I am content with weaknesses, insults, hardships, persecutions, and calamities. For when I am weak, then I am strong."

My learning disability, I now understand, was to eventually be a living demonstration to me and all who would hear me speak or read my words that God's power, not mine, is at work spreading the message He has given me. I cannot emphasize enough how difficult it still is for me to even create an email or write a speech. What takes others a few moments might take me hours. I can't memorize the Bible. I still find reading difficult. It's hard for me to study. There are so many things I still find challenging. But I do know that He has me where He wants me. This is His plan for me. And to do my part, I simply take baby steps. It's all baby steps.

So am I up to the challenge? Of course! Because God is at work, not Gina. I am enough—just as I am—because God is at work in me and through me. I am chosen. And finally, I am not ashamed. All I have to do is show up with a willing heart and take baby steps in the direction He leads. And then I get to watch what He does! Every corner I turn, I see the Lord at work.

• • •

Recently I had the privilege of speaking to about four hundred lawyers involved in Volunteer Lawyers for Justice. I told them my story and explained how changes in the law could help fight trafficking and the destruction it leaves in its wake. Lots of them lined up to speak to me afterward, but four stood out to me—one man and three women.

Each of them whispered, "I was a victim too."

Does that surprise you in a gathering like that? Remember that victimization is everywhere. Trafficking doesn't discriminate. Male. Female. Rich. Poor. Even more remarkable is that all four of them told me, "I've never told anyone before."

I encouraged each of them to stop keeping their secrets and to reach out to a counselor or mentor and break their silence so they could begin to heal.

At another event, a sweet-looking eighty-four-year-old nun approached me after my presentation at a university. Softly weeping, she whispered, "Thank you so much for sharing your story. I have to tell you, you're the first one I'm telling, but this happened to me, too." We locked eyes and, in that moment, shared a bond that only another victim can share. For her, it was a secret that no one else could hear.

One evening I took my place at the podium to speak to law enforcement personnel. My hope was to inspire them to be on the lookout for trafficking victims and to remember that often people who appear to be guilty might actually be victims themselves. As I scanned the audience, I spotted a girl in the fourth row. Next to her was a service dog. A yellow lab, I believe. It struck me as very odd that a child would be at a gathering like this. It was an evening event that started at seven o'clock, after all. Wouldn't this be a late night for her? And the subject matter seemed way too mature for one so young. I even got nervous, mentally scanning my presentation for words and concepts not meant for a child. But even though I felt uncomfortable with her presence, I had to begin.

When my presentation was over, people lined up to speak with me. One officer hung back with a woman standing at his side. After the crowd dispersed, they stepped forward.

The officer lowered his voice to say, "I have a little girl here. She's ten. This is her mother."

The woman chimed in. "Would you be willing to speak privately with my daughter? She's been going to therapy for a long time, but she won't open up to anyone. After you told your story, she said she felt like she could talk to you."

A surge of energy went through me. I knew God was at work here. The officer went on. "She was abducted and raped at the age of four. Over time she had four traffickers. Law enforcement found her when she was eight years old. You probably know how unusual it is that she was found at all. The amazing thing is that we found her traffickers, too."

I motioned for the girl to come over, and we sat down face to face. In my heart I prayed for wisdom. I patted her dog. Then she began to tell me her story.

Do you see? Every corner I turn, the Lord is there. He shows up. He is always at work in His perfect timing. And I'm always in awe when I actually feel and see Him. It's simply priceless!

ACKNOWLEDGMENTS

Looking back on my journey and considering the harm that others meant for me, I see how blessed I've been by the many people who have shown me love, walked alongside me, supported me, and believed in me. These individuals have brought me through some very difficult trials. They saw a beauty in me that I couldn't see.

To my husband, Peter: Your unconditional love, support, and encouragement have made this journey possible, and you continue to inspire me every day. You are proof of God's love for me. I am blessed to have found a husband who loves God and his family unconditionally. I will cherish and love you always.

To my beautiful daughter, Lisa: You were the miracle baby I was told I would never have. God proved the doctors wrong and blessed me to be your mother. I will always be grateful for the gift of love and joy you bring into my life. You stood by me even when I believed I fell short as a mom. I am so proud of everything you have become. Whatever you touch becomes beautiful. I will always love you.

To my beautiful grandchildren, Gianna, Joey, Vincent, Francesca, and Dominic: Thank you for your unique personalities, your joy, your laughter, and the love and hugs you bring into my life. You are a constant reminder of how God truly loves me.

Always be you, and always put the Word of God before the word of others.

To Tracy: I'm so grateful for you. I remember when you first came into my life as that sweet, precious little girl. When your chocolate ice cream cone fell onto my white sweater, I couldn't have cared less! As we both laughed, I knew how much I loved you. Stay beautiful, my unexpected second miracle daughter. I loved you then, and I always will.

To Xavier, Kali, and Zane: Though many miles separate us, the joy you bring to your mother becomes my joy as well. You have a special place in my heart.

To my beautiful cousins Giovanna, Nancy, Rita, Christine, Victoria, Alex, Megan, Richard, Julia, and Laura: Thank you for your unconditional love and unwavering support—and for showing me the true meaning of family!

To Phil: Thank you for your mentoring, spiritual guidance, and love. I'm especially thankful that we are family. Thank you for the joy you bring us and for modeling God's unconditional love.

To my church family, Phil, Lisa, Scott, John, Vinnie, Marianne, Joelle, Donna, Maggie, and Joan: God used all of you to help shape and support me through some painful times. Thank you for your dedication to this ministry and for being a vessel to help change lives. I so appreciate Lisa, Phil, Peter, Ryan, Marielle, and countless others who continually prayed for me through my health challenges, healing, and the writing of this book. *Thank you* never seems adequate! Sandra, Serge, and Adam, you have been my rock. Sandra, you gave me the idea to write this book. I will always remember how you inspired me.

To Julie and Rob Davis: This journey began one Saturday morning when our paths crossed at Emergence Church. Julie, your friendship to me has been a priceless gift, and you both have been instrumental in connecting me with Cindy. If not for your guidance, prayers, and support, *A Survivor's Secrets* would never have come to fruition. You planted the seeds that have grown into something beyond what I could have ever imagined. I will forever be grateful to the Lord for your pivotal role in this book!

To my amazing editor and collaborative writer, Cindy Lambert: What an incredible blessing the first time we met was—I felt God's presence from the start. We had many challenges along the way, but you were such an encouragement and have been so instrumental in helping shape my story. I'm looking forward to our continued journey together.

To Focus on the Family and Tyndale House Publishers, especially Vance, Kelly, John, Robin, Jennifer, Sarah, and many others: Thank you for your support and dedication, for investing the best of yourselves in this book. This would not have been possible without you all.

To my agent, Wes Yoder: Thank you for making my dream a reality. I am still pinching myself!

Thank you to my NJCAHT family: Danny, Jessica, Wincey, Caroline, Christine, Miriam, Patti, L.A., Claire, Stephen, Carol, Sheri, Catherine, Ingrid, all the Susans, Jeffrey, Louise, Janice, Roseann, Fern, Diana, Ellen, Renee, and Sister Mary Floyd. And a special thanks to Kate for all your support and all you do.

Thank you to all my friends who are now my family: Peggy, Steve, Clair, Jo, Jan, Kate, Charlie, Cindy, Mitzi, Tricia, Sandy, Jessica, Jenna, Pat, Steven, Monica, Rosario, Meghan, Jeanne, Pete, Penny, Barbara, Tom, Ellen, Darlene, Liz, Cristian, Suleman, Harold, John-Michael, Christabelle, Lamont, Taryn, Cheri, Theresa, Alicia, Connie, Toshia, Kimberly, Lennie, Kelly, Jen, Barry, Gina, Lori, Tonya, Michelle, Jo, Kir, Ashleigh, Peter, Sara, Autumn, Raeyn, Augustina, Ann Marie, and Elizabeth. And to Ursula: Words could never express my gratitude for all you did to nurse me back to health, from late nights to weekends. You tended to my needs in such practical and giving ways.

To Monica at the Beauty for Freedom project: You have been a good friend, mentor, sister, and collaborator. You have been so instrumental in helping me see the beauty I couldn't see. Thank you for the artwork you encouraged me to take part in, for participating in presentations, and more. Thank you for your passion in helping us capture our true beauty and talent. I am blessed by our friendship.

To Mitzi and Carol: Thank you for your passion and commitment in all that you do to raise awareness to help end trafficking. My life has been richly blessed by all that you do.

To my friends at NJAAP's Anti-Trafficking Task Force, Aldina, Nicole, Marlana, and Felicia: Thank you for your friendship, kindness, and support.

To my friends at Volunteer Lawyers for Justice, Jessica, Eric, Jeffrey, and Lauren: Thank you for all your help over the years. I know it's your job, but it's my life, and I feel that you all went above and beyond. The respect and professional representation you provided to me will never be forgotten.

Thank you to so many others I could not name but who contributed in some way to my journey as a survivor. I am beyond grateful!

KEEPING YOUNG PEOPLE SAFE FROM TRAFFICKING

THE UNITED STATES Department of Homeland Security defines *human trafficking* as "the use of force, fraud, or coercion to obtain some type of labor or commercial sex act."[8] Human trafficking comes in many forms and discriminates against no one. A predator will prey upon anyone's weakness regardless of age, background, or gender. Trafficking can occur anywhere and at any time. Although "force" often means physical restraint, sexual assault, or beatings, it can also include psychological coercion.

Abduction means the taking of a person against their will by means of persuasion, fraud, or force. Again, a person doesn't have to be physically picked up or forced into a vehicle in order for the event to be considered abduction. There is also psychological abduction, in which a person is manipulated to the point of losing his or her control over their own will and choices.

Traffickers are often masters at deception and manipulation. They mislead victims with false hopes, promises, and attractive opportunities that never happen. Victims are pulled into trafficking because they believe they will be provided with prospective jobs to help improve their income and financial conditions.

Red Flags

A child, teen, or adult may be (or have been) a trafficking victim if they

- become secretive or tell you that someone has asked them to keep a secret;
- decrease or change their communication habits;
- act as if they are being controlled;
- indicate that they are not free to come and go as they wish;
- respond to you with seemingly rehearsed answers;
- lack control of earned money (teen or adult);
- do not have control over their own identification documents (teen or adult);
- avoid eye contact;
- become unusually defensive or argumentative;
- seem to mistrust individuals displaying compassion;
- have tattoos or scarring of trafficker's name and/or symbols;
- have visible signs of sexual violence, physical restraint, or confinement;
- seem malnourished, exhausted, or sleep deprived; and/or
- begin dressing inappropriately.

Trust your gut. When your gut is saying something feels wrong, it *is* wrong. You don't need to ask others. If it looks wrong, it is wrong. If you're feeling those butterflies or uneasiness inside you, that's another red flag!

How to Be a Safe Zone

Even excellent parents could have a child, of any age, tricked into becoming a victim of trafficking. But remember that the safer your children feel with you, the less vulnerable they will be to predators.

Cultivate these six characteristics in your family so that your child will feel that you are always their "safe zone."

1. Build a loving and nurturing home environment, making sure your child feels loved above all else. Respect your child, believe their words, and ensure you give them no cause to fear you. Because if they live in fear, they're going to be afraid to come to you.

2. Engage in good, healthy, open communication with your child and reinforce the fact that they can safely tell you anything.

3. Encourage your child not to keep secrets and explain that secrets are not safe. You must prove to your child through example that if they tell you the truth you will not shame or punish them. Teach them the saying "You are as sick as your secrets" and that secrets lead to fear and shame.

4. Regularly educate your child about the reality and danger of predators and the importance of never going anywhere with or confiding in a stranger. Reinforce these ideas each year as your child grows older and understands more. (Use the lists in this section.) As you teach them about potential dangers, help them clearly understand these terms: *boundaries*, *respect*, and *consent*.

   Boundaries are limits. To set healthy boundaries means to set wise limits on behavior toward you that you will accept or tolerate.

   Respect means regard for the feelings and wishes and abilities of a person. *Self-respect* means care and concern and regard for your own feelings, wishes, and abilities.

   Consent means voluntary participation in or agreement to or approval of an act or a willingness to take part.

5. Cultivate in yourself and your child an awareness of the people in your neighborhood and the larger environment surrounding you at all times.

6. Notice if your child seems nervous or upset or acting in any unusual ways, and gently probe to find out why. Keep in mind that some things may be too difficult for them to articulate in words and so they might begin to act out. Stay calm as they communicate, even if your child is upset, so that they feel safe enough to express themselves.

Children with Phones and Computers

In a world where kids and teens feel entitled to own a smartphone or laptop with limitless access to the internet, establish a few guidelines to help keep them safe.

- Have open conversation about the dangers, risks, and reality of online predators.
- Remove all electronic devices from your child's bedroom—day or night—until you know they are able to make responsible decisions.
- Keep all electronics and phones out of bedrooms at night, no matter how responsible you believe they are.
- Always be aware of the people and groups of people your child or teen is communicating with.
- Place reasonable, age-appropriate limits on time spent on phones and computers.
- Use parental controls on devices to monitor or limit tech use to a few trusted apps and websites. There is no need to give your child total access to everything available on the internet.
- Make sure you know your child's passwords.

- Have your child or teen keep their phone charged and have a charger with them when they leave home.
- Use the tracking services on your teen's phone so you know their location when they are away from the house.

Safety Training for Parents

Again, trust your gut. You don't need to ask permission. Follow your instincts. And teach your child or teen to tell a parent or someone in authority when they are feeling uneasy or unsafe.

- Never force the child to hug or kiss someone if they feel reluctant to do so, even if it's a family member.
- Correct or discipline in private, never in public. Doing so in front of others invites others to shame the child and diminishes the child's self-respect.
- As your child grows, continue to reinforce the importance of boundaries, respect, and consent.
- Together with your child or teen, come up with a secret word that they are only to use with you if they are sensing trouble or are in trouble.
- Know who your child or teen is with at all times.
- Have the phone numbers and addresses of your child's or teen's friends and their parents.
- Always know where your child is, who they are with, and how they are getting home. If they are staying overnight at a friend's home, speak to the parent yourself.
- Take your teen to where they are going and pick them up. Offer to give rides to their friends' homes.
- Be involved in their school activities.
- Listen for what your child *isn't* telling you.

- Use discipline rather than punishment. Don't scare your child or teen with punishment. You don't want your child to fear you but to respect you. Remember that punishment lasts a short time and wise discipline lasts a lifetime!
- Invite your child or teen to talk with you about anything without fear. If they can't come to you, if you don't create a safe space and believe them, they will go to someone else—and that someone else may be a predator at some level.
- In smaller matters, allow your child to think for themselves and to learn about choices and the consequences of those choices. Encourage them to create their own style and choose the colors, music, and hobbies they enjoy. Be their champion. Help them discover the positive and negative consequences of their choices and how that is a major part of developing healthy friendships and other relationships.
- Help your child or teen see their gifts and identify parts of their character that could be assets or that could be liabilities that might hurt them or someone else.
- Don't shame your child or teen.
- Be a role model and lead by example.
- Affirm your child and teen frequently. Affirmation teaches self-respect and autonomy.
- When out and about visiting places, always arrange a meeting point for you and your child or teen in case either of you gets lost.
- Make sure you are all together or have seats close together when traveling on a train, bus, or plane.
- Always go with a younger child into public restrooms.

Safety Training for Children and Teens

Teach your child to trust their gut—that when their gut is feeling like something is wrong or looks wrong, it is wrong—and that they don't need to ask others. Explain that if they are feeling butterflies inside, that is a red flag! Teach them to tell a parent or someone in authority what they are feeling.

- Teach your child healthy boundaries for physical touch.
- Have your child memorize your phone number and address and your first and last name.
- Let your child know not to go into bathrooms or private rooms alone when out with friends. They should always have a buddy and stick with them.
- Teach your child that it is wise to scream if they are feeling uncomfortable, unsafe, or scared.
- Teach and demonstrate how to be aware of their surroundings and the people near them because human trafficking can come in many different forms.
- Help your child come up with a secret word that they are only to use with you if they are in trouble.
- Teach your child that if they get lost, they should stay where they are and ask for help from a police officer, another grown-up with children, or someone working at a nearby shop.
- Teach your child not to share personal information online.
- Teach your child to respect places and things that look dangerous and to be alert to potential danger.
- Teach your child that their body is theirs alone.
- Teach your child to never keep secrets.

- Teach your child to report suspicious activity.
- Teach your child to avoid talking to people they don't know when you're not around.
- Make sure your child knows never to walk away with strangers or anyone they may feel uncomfortable with even if they do know them.
- Make sure your child or teen understands that they should always tell you if a stranger or someone they know approaches them or asks them to keep a secret.
- If your child or teen is traveling alone, tell them to sit near other families on the train or bus.
- Avoid having your child use a lift or car service or tell them only to do so with friends. If your child or teen must use one, they should not hesitate to get out if they are uncomfortable about someone else being there.
- If a child or teen is uncomfortable staying at a friend's home or a party, assure them they can always call home for a ride. They should never be afraid or ashamed of calling home to get picked up.
- Encourage your child or teen to speak up if they are being bullied or feel they might be in danger.
- Especially for teens, encourage them to find a safe and trusted adult to speak to even if it's not a parent. Perhaps it could be a teacher or school counselor or youth director or pastor.
- Always let your child know that they can come to you for anything and that they will never be shamed or need to be afraid.

A Special Note about Teen Dating Violence

Unhealthy, abusive, or violent relationships can have short- and long-term negative effects, including severe effects, on a developing teen. Youth who are victims of teen dating violence are more likely to

- experience depression and anxiety symptoms;
- engage in unhealthy behaviors, such as using tobacco, drugs, and alcohol;
- exhibit antisocial behaviors, such as lying, theft, bullying, or hitting; and
- think about suicide.

Violence in an adolescent relationship sets the stage for future relationship problems, including intimate partner violence and sexual violence perpetration and/or victimization throughout life. For example, youth who are victims of dating violence in high school are at higher risk for victimization during college.

A Special Note about Shaming

Don't laugh at or mock others, and don't seek to humiliate or embarrass them. Doing so is disrespectful and harmful, and if you're doing this to your kids or friends, you are teaching them to be disrespectful to others. When this is done, you are humiliating that person and shaming them. They are not listening to what you are trying to tell them, because shame has just taken over every part of them.

Shaming does not preserve the dignity and respect of that child, and it turns what could have been an effective teachable moment into a destructive incident. It is putting that child at risk by giving permission to other siblings or classmates or those who are listening to criticize that child for what they did. If your goal is to correct the child and coach them to make better choices, do so in private and in a respectful manner.

A Special Note about Discipline and Punishment

Although I believe children need discipline in their lives, this is different from punishment. Punishment can destroy and crush a child with fear and shame, and it often teaches them behavior that is not healthy. Also, punishment lasts for a short time, but discipline can last a lifetime.

Incorporating natural consequences is more effective than unrelated punishment, as is suspending privileges such as watching shows and using electronic devices. We must remember the messages we are sending to our children when we discipline them. What lessons are they learning about how they should treat other people? We always want to be mindful of keeping respect at the forefront of everything we say and do.

Meeting your child with love and acceptance and nurturing them to make better choices should be your goal. This will equip them with tools to feel confident to trust their judgment and make good, sound decisions and will more likely have a positive outcome. In so doing, you will be teaching and modeling valuable survivor tools.

A Special Note about Sibling Issues

I'll sometimes hear a parent say, "Oh, the kids are just fighting. It's just normal sibling rivalry." Or maybe "They just play rough. It's who they are." Parents must recognize that physical or psychological mistreatment cannot be considered to be normal or acceptable.

Don't compare or continually give more attention and value

to one sibling over the other. It creates low self-esteem with a child and causes resentment between siblings. Be on guard to never allow a child in your family to be bullied or victimized by a sibling. When this occurs, be certain to do the following:

- Intervene as soon as possible.
- Discipline the bully.
- Have the bully apologize to the victim.
- Teach the bully to value the bullied child.
- Affirm the value of the bullied child and make a plan to emphasize their value and worth.
- Set the example of acceptable behavior. Don't tease, don't criticize. When you tease and criticize, the impact that it leaves on an individual is incredibly powerful.

Note: Girls need to learn how to be treated by boys, and boys need to learn how to treat girls. Do not permit inappropriate touching or abusive behavior of any kind.

A Special Note to Teachers

I know you probably want to choose the brilliant kids in your class who always have their hands up and always have the right answers. That's certainly a rewarding feeling and may very well be a positive reflection on you as a teacher. My heart, however, is with those children who always have the wrong answers, who are laughed at and criticized, and who may very well be the children you find distracting because they are the class clowns. (Many of us use humor to hide behind our pain.)

These are often the students who are not connected to any- one or anything, perhaps because no one at home has connected with them. They may not know how to connect appropriately.

I was one of those children—the troublemakers, those who are disrespectful, don't pay attention, always fall asleep in class, and never have their homework turned in. Even the bullies may fall into this lot. Have we thought about the pain they are hiding behind? Working with these individuals may be your most difficult challenge because there are clearly underlying issues that may not be their fault. They are likely not confident or thriving.

I believe you can be the person who literally changes the trajectory of that child's life. You are holding their future in your hands. Be the person who seeks the good in them and helps them recognize that they have value and hope, that they are worth investing in and are seen and heard.

Be that safe person and safe space for them to help find their gifts and grow.

Where to Turn for Help

If you are in the United States and believe someone may be a victim of human trafficking, call the 24-hour National Human Trafficking Hotline at (888) 373-7888 or text HELP to BeFree (233733). If you or someone you know is in immediate danger, call 911.

To report someone suspected of human trafficking to law enforcement, dial (866) 347-2423 to submit a report to the US Homeland Security tip line, which is available twenty-four hours a day, seven days a week. Highly trained specialists take reports from both the public and law enforcement agencies on possible violations of more than four hundred laws, including those related to human trafficking. Outside the United States, the tip line is accessible by calling (802) 872-6199. This information and more is available at dhs.gov/blue-campaign/identify-victim.

For more information and help, visit the following organizations:

- AllianceToEndHumanTrafficking.org (Alliance to End Human Trafficking)
- MissingKids.org (National Center for Missing & Exploited Children)
- ECPAT.org (ECPAT)
- 988lifeline.org (National Suicide & Crisis Lifeline)
- SharedHope.org (Shared Hope International)

NOTES

1. Stephen J. Dubner, "Frank Warren Spills His Secrets," Freakonomics, October 18, 2007, https://freakonomics.com/2007/10/frank-warren -spills-his-secrets.
2. "The Twelve Steps," Alcoholics Anonymous, accessed April 12, 2023, https://www.aa.org/the-twelve-steps.
3. New Jersey Commission on Human Trafficking, *Annual Report 2020* (Trenton, NJ: New Jersey Division of Criminal Justice, 2020), https://www .nj.gov/oag/dcj/humantrafficking/downloads/HT-Commsission-2020-Final -Report.pdf.
4. John Baker, *Getting Right with God, Yourself, and Others—Participant's Guide 3: A Recovery Program Based on Eight Principles from the Beatitudes (Celebrate Recovery)*, rev. ed. (Grand Rapids, MI: Zondervan, 2012).
5. Glenn Patrick Doyle, "Ironically, when we start to get better, we also often get sad," Twitter, June 14, 2021, 9:00 p.m., https://twitter.com/DrDoyleSays /status/1404604572128059394.
6. "The 2023 Florida Statutes (including 2022 Special Session A and 2023 Special Session B)," Online Sunshine, accessed April 12, 2023, http://www .leg.state.fl.us/statutes/index.cfm?App_mode=Display_Statute&URL=0900 -0999/0943/Sections/0943.0583.html.
7. "Theresa Flores—Founder of the SOAP Project," SOAP Project, accessed April 12, 2023, https://www.soapproject.org/theresa-flores.
8. "What is Human Trafficking?" Blue Campaign, Department of Homeland Security, https://www.dhs.gov/blue-campaign/what-human-trafficking.

FOCUS ON THE FAMILY.

We're here for you

AT EVERY STAGE OF LIFE

Single or married. No kids or several. Just starting out, or in your golden years. Whatever life looks like, we've got something for you. Find books, articles, podcasts, and more for wherever you are in your journey.

Find it all here
FocusOnTheFamily.com

FOCUS ON THE FAMILY.

KNOW SOMEONE THAT NEEDS HELP?

You can reach out for help. Talk to someone – at no cost to you.

Call Today
1-855-771-HELP (4357)

Find help here
FocusOnTheFamily.com/gethelp